STRATEGY AND COMPUTERS:
Information Systems as Competitive Weapons

STRATEGY
AND
COMPUTERS:
Information Systems as
Competitive Weapons

CHARLES WISEMAN

DOW JONES-IRWIN   Homewood, IL 60430

© DOW JONES-IRWIN, 1985

This publication is designed to provide accurate and
authoritative information in regard to the subject matter
covered. It is sold with the understanding that neither the author
nor the publisher is engaged in rendering legal, accounting, or
other professional service. If legal advice or other expert
assistance is required, the services of a competent
professional person should be sought.

*From a Declaration of Principles jointly adopted by a Committee
of the American Bar Association and a Committee of Publishers.*

ISBN 0-87094-590-4

Library of Congress Catalog Card No. 85-70567

Printed in the United States of America

1 2 3 4 5 6 7 8 9 0 K 2 1 0 9 8 7 6 5

To MBW

Preface

I began collecting instances of information systems used for strategic purposes five years ago, dubbing them *strategic information systems* (SIS). But from the start, I was puzzled by their occurrence. At least theoretically, I was unprepared to admit the existence of a new variety of computer application. The conventional view at the time recognized only management information systems and management support systems, the former used to automate basic business processes and the latter to satisfy the information needs of decision makers.

But as my file of cases grew, I realized that the conventional perspective on information systems was incomplete, unable to account for SIS. The examples belied the theory, and the theory in general blinded believers from seeing SIS. Indeed, some conventional information system planning methodologies, which act like theories in guiding the systematic search for computer application opportunities, explicitly exclude certain SIS possibilities from what might be found.

This growing awareness of the inadequacy of the dominant dogma of the day led me to investigate the conceptual foundations, so to speak, of information systems. At first, I believed that the conventional gospel could be enlarged to accommodate SIS. But as my research progressed, I abandoned this position and concluded that to explain SIS and facilitate their discovery, one needed to view applications of computer technology from a radically different vantage point.

I call this the *strategic perspective* on information systems. The chapters to follow present my conception of it. Written primarily for top executives and line managers, they show how computers can be used to support or shape competitive strategy.

While this book may have its theoretical moments, it is intended primarily to be a practical guide. The best way to grasp the strategic perspective is by studying actual cases of SIS in an analytical framework that illuminates their significance. Since this is not a textbook, I have suppressed the usual scholarly apparatus, but readers with an academic bent will find at the end of each chapter a list of case references and a bibliography of works that record my intellectual debts.

The use of information systems as competitive weapons and the relation between strategy and computers are new topics of inquiry. As far as I know, there are no books devoted specifically to these subjects. While I take a certain pleasure in being the first to publish, no one knows better than myself the limits of the present formulation. But whatever the shortcomings of my conception, the book's purpose will be served if practitioners, academics, and others who wish to understand how computers can be used to gain advantage, can be persuaded to adopt a strategic perspective on information systems, even if it differs from the one proposed here.

My obligations in this venture are numerous. In particular, I want to thank Ian MacMillan, professor of management and director of the Center for Entrepreneurial Studies at the New York University Graduate School of Management. He encouraged me to write a paper for the *Journal of Business Strategy* on the strategic uses of information systems. An early draft, which he sent to the publisher, led to a contract for this book. A number of friends read the entire manuscript and greatly improved it by their comments: Nick Rackoff and Al Ullrich of GTE, Jerry Kanter and Frank Chen of Honeywell Information Systems, and Bill Heuser of Abex. Others read or discussed parts of it with me and made valuable suggestions: Mel Fleisher, John James, Mal Nechis, and Dick Rutledge of

IBM, Randy Drummond of GE, Ralph Loftin of Ralph Loftin Associates Group, and Liam Fahey of the Kellogg Graduate School of Business (Northwestern University).

Charles Wiseman

Contents

1

Strategic Information Systems

PERSPECTIVES ON INFORMATION SYSTEMS

What we see is largely determined by what we believe. For centuries, Chinese astronomers identified stars, planets, and comets undetected by their Western counterparts. Neither the availability of powerful optical instruments nor the location, anatomy, or physiology of the scientists accounts for these instances of celestial vision and blindness. Rather, the explanation resides in the radically different perspectives from which these two groups viewed the universe.

When Western astronomers scanned the sky, they expected to see nothing new. They were religious men who believed the bodies in God's heaven to be fixed and immutable. The Chinese, on the other hand, adhered to cosmological ideas that did not preclude celestial change and novelty. Evidence that these different perspectives shaped the horizon of expectation, the mental set of those who adopted them, emerged in the late 16th century when the religious dogma was overthrown. Western observers then recorded for the first time what the Chinese had seen hundreds of years earlier. Fitted with a different pair of conceptual glasses, they saw objects previously invisible to them.

The ability to see requires more than eyes. Identifying information systems—like discovering stars, planets, and comets—depends on our conceptual perspective. From one vantage point, we see some information system varieties and miss others. Change that point, and we perceive a radically different system space. If a firm's destiny hinges on its use of computer technology, it had better view information systems from the proper perspective.

But what is the proper perspective? As the pace of competition intensifies in the 80s, this has become a critical question for many enterprises. Yet whatever the answer, one thing is clear. The reigning dogma on the organizational uses of information systems won't do. And the firm that fails to rethink its use of computer technology may find itself at risk.

This, unfortunately, seems to be the position of an increasingly large number of firms today. Since the advent of data processing in the mid-50s, one viewpoint has exclusively dominated their thinking about information system opportunities. It holds that the organizational purpose served by computer applications is either (1) to automate a basic process (subprocess or task) or (2) to provide information for decision making. It is concerned primarily with information flows, data bases, and the production of reports related to the organization's planning and control operations. I call this the *conventional perspective* on information systems.

A data processing professional exemplified it in the early 70s when he advocated a new approach for information systems planning, a top-down method "to focus on the critical tasks and decisions made within an organization and to provide the kind of information that the manager needs to perform those tasks and make those decisions." The author of a recent book on the health care industry reflects it when he asserts that "the only computer services that a hospital really needs—the basic financial, billing, and accounting operations—could be purchased relatively inexpensively from any service company."

When adherents of the conventional perspective search for information system opportunities, they look for two varieties: *management information systems* (MIS) and *management support systems* (MSS). (MSS includes as its two main species: *decision support systems* and *executive information systems*.) These varieties are intended to serve organizational purposes associated with the conventional perspective, that is, automating basic processes (the domain of MIS) and satisfying the information needs of managers and professionals, needs often closely connected with planning and control decisions (the domain of MSS).

But the conventional perspective, important as it is for identifying and illuminating the significance of thse two varieties, offers too limited a view of the world of information systems.*

Consider, for example, how Metpath Inc. uses systems to compete in the tough, fragmented clinical laboratory industry, where low differentiation of service has led to a lack of customer loyalty and frequent price discounting. Doctors send specimens to the lab

---

*Readers interested in an evolutionary account of the conventional perspective on information systems should refer to Appendix A.

for processing and in return expect timely, accurate analyses. Metpath enhanced its customer service by installing computer terminals in doctors' offices and linking them to its lab computers. For a small monthly fee, physicians receive test results as soon as they are determined.

From the conventional vantage point, the system might be seen as a transaction-processing, on-line database application providing critical diagnostic information to physicians. But this description captures neither its competitive import nor its innovative character. By changing conceptual lenses and viewing it from a *strategic perspective*, we see it as an attempt by Metpath to use its information system as a double-edged sword.

First, it builds barriers against new and existing rivals by raising the information systems ante. Second, it enables Metpath to gain an edge over other labs by differentiating an otherwise commodity service. Metpath keeps historical records of patient data on file and offers its customers computerized processing services for billing and accounts payable operations, as well as easy access to stock market quotations from the Dow Jones network. Finally, the system can expand the services it offers into such areas as diagnosis (when expert systems become available) and drug interaction testing. Referring to the latter, the vice president for scientific affairs of the American Pharmaceutical Association said: "If there is such a thing as the wave of the future, this is it." Primed as it is to store patient profile data on such items as drug and food allergies, chronic illnesses, and medications taken, the Metpath system will permit physicians to conduct drug interaction tests prior to writing prescriptions. Each of these information system-based hooks serve to differentiate a commodity service and thereby secure the loyalty of the estimated one in five doctors who switch annually from lab to lab in search of lower prices.

The conventional perspective on information systems supplies scant guidance to those who wish to discover such application opportunities or explain their strategic impact. Nor is it of much help in accounting for the extended uses made by American and United Airlines of their computerized reservation systems, Sabre and Apollo, respectively. Built in the 70s at a cost of over $250 million each, these information systems are no longer employed merely as neutral scheduling mechanisms to automate the seat reservation process. Rather, they are being used increasingly as weapons in the struggle for industry domination.

Sabre and Apollo give priority listing to American and United flights when travel agents request information on their computer terminals. An agent who uses the Sabre system and requests a listing of flights from New York to Los Angeles with stops in between knows that the first few items to appear on the screen may not show the most direct way, nor the least expensive way, but for sure they'll show the American way.

American and United have used their reservation systems to virtually preempt the major channel of distribution. In the computerized travel agency market, they form a powerful duopoly with shares of 41 percent and 39 percent, respectively. The crumbs (the remaining 20 percent) have been left to the competition. While Delta, Eastern, and TWA have developed smaller systems to limit their exposure, the other carriers are at risk. As one of the less fortunate put it: "We clearly didn't pay enough attention, and now its a direct threat." Over 80 percent of the nation's 20,000 travel agencies, accounting for 90 percent of airline ticket sales, are computerized. In regions where the airline with the reservation system has numerous flights, the prioritization procedure can lead to as much as 20 percent more revenue.

In addition, Sabre and Apollo have become vehicles of diversification and growth, propelling American and United into new lines of business. According to the president of American, "This industry needs every cent it can generate. We've got to be creative about using our huge asset base to develop new revenues. We're looking at businesses we can be in at low costs because some of the links are already in place."

These links form, in American's words, "the world's most powerful nonmilitary computer system." According to the vice president of marketing and automation systems at American, 65,000 devices hang off the network, which runs 23 hours a day, 365 days a year, and keeps track of 6.5 million domestic and international airfare combinations, more than 10,000 daily fare changes, and the schedules of about 650 airlines around the world. In 1983, for example, it handled over 55 million calls at its four reservation centers. To exploit excess capacity on Sabre, the carrier recently formed American Airlines Telemarketing Services. AATS performs services such as conducting marketing surveys and taking pledges generated by telethons. The fee income from these operations, American expects, will be supplemented in the future when it uses its net to offer consumer products to home computer users.

The two cases just described are instances of *strategic information systems* (SIS), information systems used to support or shape the competitive strategy of the organization. SIS represents a new information system variety, radically different in organizational use from those countenanced by the conventional perspective.*

The conventional perspective is unsuited for guiding the systematic search for SIS opportunities, and is incapable of explaining the strategic significance of applications. Like the Western astronomers unprepared to see new celestial objects, believers in the conventional gospel on information systems are unable to discern most SIS opportunities. Lying still further beyond the conventional field of vision, the entire spectrum of strategic alliances supported or shaped by information systems also goes undetected.

Paine Webber, for instance, seized an alliance opportunity in 1984 that no other brokerage house had previously been able to capture. It negotiated a pact with the State Street Bank and Trust Company of Boston enabling it to participate in MasterTeller, the nationwide automated teller network run for banks by Master-Card International, a credit card and traveler's check organization owned by 24,000 banks and other institutions. The MasterTeller network lets cardholders withdraw cash from the over 1,500 automated teller machines scattered throughout the United States.

Up to this time, banks had been very careful to exclude rivals offering competitive financial services from entry to their networks. Indeed, two of the largest bank-owned nationwide nets, the Plus and Cirrus systems, rejected requests from Merrill Lynch and

---

*Readers interested in relating the emergence of SIS to the conventional MIS and MSS varieties should refer to Appendix B.

the Fidelity Group, a Boston-based mutual fund company, to establish similar arrangements.

Now Paine Webber customers can use credit cards issued by State Street to get the same 24-hour access to cash that bank cardholders enjoy. Because of this alliance, a cardholder with a Paine Webber account can withdraw money at automatic teller machines across the country. The story of how Paine Webber will use this new alliance in packaging its products has yet to unfold. In any case, the deal illustrates how the broker capitalized on information systems assets *developed by others* to serve its own strategic ends.

Another form of strategic alliance involving information systems is illustrated by a recent joint venture. IBM and Merrill Lynch announced in 1984 the formation of International MarketNet, a new information service intended to provide users of IBM PCs with stock quotations, investment data, analytical processing, financial software, and so on. The service will enable end users to communicate via satellite links with Merrill's host computers. Monchik-Weber, a software house specializing in the securities industry and acquired by McGraw-Hill after International MarketNet opened its doors, won the contract to develop the systems that will run the service.

International MarketNet is a 50–50 joint venture alliance between IBM and Merrill Lynch. The venture's customers will be drawn from Merrill's 10,000 account representatives, other brokerage houses, commercial banks, money managers, and clients of these firms. For IBM, the alliance supports its strategy of market expansion; for Merrill, its plans to diversify into the information services industry and to reduce and eventually eliminate the fees it now pays to Quotron Systems, Inc. for the use of its stock-quotation system. (Currently, 25 percent of Quotron's customers are employees of Merrill.)

The two cases just described involve instances of *strategic information system alliances*, intra- or interorganizational combinations in which information system assets are used to support or shape the competitive strategy of the organization. Since, by definition, systems so used are strategic information systems, remarks which follow about SIS opportunities (unless otherwise noted) should be taken to apply to SIS alliance opportunities as well.

These SIS alliances, as well as the SIS examples detailed earlier, exemplify the strategic use of information systems. Representing instances in which competitive strategy is supported or shaped by the application of computer technology, they mark a dramatic turning in the brief evolutionary history of information systems. But to appreciate more deeply this break with the past, this movement from the conventional to the strategic, requires something more than the trotting out of SIS cases. What we need to show are examples of firms that have developed a vision of information systems to guide their strategic course.

STRATEGIC INFORMATION SYSTEM VISION

To see that an information system application *is* a SIS, we need to understand how information systems are used to support or shape the firm's competitive strategy. This ability to see and understand I call *strategic information system vision.*

A firm with a powerful SIS vision zealously encourages the search for opportunities to use information systems to gain a competitive edge. And when they are discovered, it marshalls the proper resources to support them. In some cases, SIS vision develops into an *image* of the future that top management uses to navigate the firm's strategic path.

How can we determine whether a firm possesses SIS vision? The best test, I believe, is to examine what the firm says and does. If it purports to appreciate the strategic significance of information systems and if it launches thrusts supported or shaped by systems, we are justified in believing that SIS vision is operating. Admittedly, this is only a rough guide. It would be preferable, to be sure, to explore from within, to observe in detail the strategic decision-making process and how information systems are woven into the fabric of strategic programs, before making a judgment.

But until interdisciplinary studies (involving business strategists, line managers, information systems professionals, and leading-edge firms) are conducted in the strategic use of computer technology, we must content ourselves with establishing indirectly, through whatever evidence can be mustered, whether an enterprise possesses SIS vision.

This is the approach I have followed in assembling the facts on Dun & Bradstreet, McKesson, and Banc One—the three firms discussed below—to support my contention that each possesses its own highly developed and successful SIS vision, a vision that guides its strategic destiny.

Dun & Bradstreet

D&B traces its origin back to 1841 when Louis Tappan, a New York dry-goods jobber, founded the Mercantile Agency, the first credit-reporting firm in the United States. Within a decade, the Bradstreet Agency became the second company to enter the field. By 1890, Mercantile (now run by R. G. Dun) had established 69 branch offices in major business centers. Being the first two firms to create nationwide networks, Bradstreet and Dun dominated the credit-reporting business. In the 1870s, Dun employed over 10,000 reporters or investigators and received some 5,000 requests a day for information. In 1930, the two firms merged to form Dun & Bradstreet.

By 1978, D&B had become a $763 million diversified information services company with four major divisions:

- Business Information Services (D&B Credit, D&B Commercial Collection, D&B International, D&B Group Life and Health Insurance Administration)
- Publishing (Reuben H. Donnelley, Official Airline Guides, Moody's Investors Service, Technical Publishing, Funk & Wagnalls)
- Marketing Services (Donnelley Marketing, Dun's Marketing, International Marketing)
- Broadcasting (Corinthian Broadcasting's Television Stations, TVS Television Network)

Business Information Services contributed 38 percent of the revenues and 27 percent of the operating income.

In 1979, D&B recorded its best year ever and made two significant strategic moves. It purchased for $164 million National CSS (NCSS), a leading computer services company with a nationwide, 80,000-mile time-sharing network, and agreed to acquire its sixth television station together with half a dozen small cable systems, giving D&B its first hands-on experience in the growing cable industry. The NCSS acquisition became part of D&B's Business Information Service Division while the television station and cable systems were to become part of the Broadcasting group.

D&B saw these moves as consistent with its strategic vision:

> There are three principal resources that are central to the continued success of the Dun & Bradstreet Corporation: our ability to collect timely and relevant *information* for the decision-making use of our various customer groups; our capacity for applying *technology* effectively to maximize information delivery and utility; and the *management* to anticipate the needs of our customers and, in partnership with our highly skilled people, to provide quality products and services worldwide.[1]

At the close of 1983, D&B had become a $1.5 billion information services giant. The contribution of the Business Information Services Division had risen in four years to 45 percent of total revenue and 34 percent of operating income. During the year, D&B made two significant strategic moves. It acquired McCormack & Dodge, a major software company specializing in financial and human resources packages, and departed from the broadcasting industry by selling its stations and systems. In 1984, D&B underlined its focus on business services and information by acquiring, through merger (a $1.08 billion stock transaction), A. C. Nielsen Company, the nation's leading consumer research concern.

D&B's recent evolutionary history, I claim, reflects SIS vison. D&B's management has executed strategic moves supported or shaped by information systems, moves that serve to support or shape D&B's long-term objective of concentrating its efforts and resources in the business services and information industry.

In 1979, Robert Weissman (NCSS's president when it was acquired by D&B and, since 1980, D&B's executive vice president and now its president and chief operating officer) proclaimed:

> NCSS and the Dun & Bradstreet Corporation are the best fit in the information industry—data from D&B operating companies plus NCSS leadership in computer services. We're going to rewrite the book on combining information and technology to develop new products for our customers.[2]

The battle cry voiced by Weissman is reflected in the following thrusts made during the 1979–84 period (including the NCSS acquisition):

Acquisition of NCSS. This major diversification move enabled D&B to enter the time-sharing business, a new market pioneered by NCSS, and to exploit NCSS's information system resources (its hardware, software, and highly skilled work force) synergistically. Within a few months after the acquisition, 12 joint projects were initiated, among them Duns Vue, a new credit product, and Moody's Municipal Credit Report Service, both designed for electronic delivery over NCSS's network. But NCSS's time-sharing business has been a disappointment. As demand declined over the past five years, due primarily to the rapid spread of microcomputer processing, D&B has had to find new uses for its valuable NCSS resources.

Acquisition of McCormack & Dodge. Like the NCSS purchase, this SIS alliance illustrates a major diversification move with a dual purpose. D&B expects to exploit M&D's software, systems know-how, and 3,000-customer base synergistically across its various product lines. And it expects M&D, an established leader in its market niche, to continue its impressive growth. Already, joint projects are emerging between M&D and D&B's other units. M&D recently introduced a new product, PC–Link, that allow users of IBM's PC to retrieve and transfer mainframe data. This product ties directly to one of D&B's newest products, DunsPlus, which is itself the result of efforts by an NCSS division (now called D&B Computing Services) and an SIS alliance struck between D&B and IBM (see below).

Acquisition of Nielsen. In the case of the NCSS and M&D acquisitions, D&B exploited the information systems assets of others. With the Nielsen merger, on the other hand, D&B saw opportunities to exploit its own information system assets. Here, there are both economy-of-scale (possible consolidation of information system services) and economy-of-scope opportunities, which have yet to unfold.

Development of Official Airline Guide/Electronic Edition. D&B's OAGs provide information on North American, Worldwide, and Air Cargo flights. In 1983, D&B announced an electronic version of these guides. The OAG/Electronic Edition can be accessed by computer terminals. It lists the information contained in the print editions, as well as fares. Users can query the flight data base for comparative fare information within specified arrival or departure periods and for lowest fares between two points. The OAG/EE, however, does not handle reservations. D&B distributes its product directly or through such information networks as Compu-Serve, Dialcom, Dow Jones News/Retrieval, Bell Canada, and Viewdata.

The OAG/EE is an instance of an innovative strategic maneuver targeted at customers who wish to reduce their travel costs, the third fastest rising corporate expense. In the past, travelers generally relied on agents for such information and, depending on the reservation system used by the agent, received flight alternatives giving priority to the airline providing the system. Now, with OAG/EE, travelers can get objective data, favoring only the airlines with the lowest prices. Soon the system will also include international fares as well as hotel and car rental rates.

Creation of DunsPlus. By forming SIS alliances with IBM, Lotus Corp., and Softword Systems, D&B created a unique product complementing its other offerings as well as providing a standalone, integrated professional workstation. DunsPlus consists of an IBM PC (D&B forged an agreement with IBM to act as a value-added remarketer), spreadsheet (Lotus 1–2–3) and word-processing (MultiMate) programs, and specifically developed D&B software (from NCSS) outfitting end users with electronic mail, file maintenance, data integration, and other capabilities. As incentives to purchase DunsPlus, D&B includes as standard features one year's sign-up charges for Western Union's electronic mail service and its own OAG/EE. Use of DunsPlus, need it be said, also makes access to D&B's extensive collection of electronic data bases, and others as well, a relatively straightforward procedure.

Built into the offering, in addition, is a micro-to-mainframe utility program called PC–Link, developed by McCormack & Dodge, which allows PC users to transmit and receive data from corporate data bases. Within the first six months after its introduction in January 1984, DunsPlus had attracted over 50 major corporate customers. One of these, the vice president and treasurer of Olin Corp., testified to the usefulness of D&B's new integrated product by saying, "I don't see why anyone would order anything else."

Development of DunsNet.   This recent D&B offering is a packet-switched telecommunications network, similar in function to General Telephone & Electronics Corporation's (GTE's) Telenet and Tymshare's Tymnet. With DunsNet, D&B offers its customers value-added networking services and distributed processing through the use of such microcomputer systems as DunsPlus. NCSS and other D&B units can also make use of the net.

DunsNet enables all D&B users to access its data bases using one standard procedure. It reduces D&B-generated revenues for Telenet and Tymnet. DunsNet represents a strategic growth move for D&B, a kind of forward integration that takes the company a step further toward its goal of being a full-service provider of information services and data to its clients.

From this short selection of strategic actions taken over a five-year period, it seems evident that D&B possesses SIS vision. If it didn't, how else can we account for such efforts to use information systems to support strategy. The reader may object that since D&B is an information services company, each of the moves cited is natural and has nothing to do with SIS vision.

But this objection is not persuasive. D&B had choices. It wasn't forced to acquire M&D or Nielson. It wasn't bullied into forming an alliance with IBM to market the PC and build a product around it. DunsNet was not inevitable. Different data-rich firms have made different strategic thrusts, some emphasizing information systems, others not. D&B itself didn't have such a clear vision of its future in 1979, as indicated by its broadcasting acquisitions. After the acquisition of NCSS, however, the die seems to have been cast, with Weissman probably sounding the clarion call.

The current evolution of D&B, inspired by SIS vision, is far from complete. By the end of this decade, in all likelihood, it should emerge as one of the leading information services firms in the world, providing a full line of products supported or shaped by information systems. The examples cited above are just the tip of the iceberg; economy-of-scope (see Chapter 4) opportunities, among others, have yet to be exploited to the fullest.

McKesson

Another example of a firm that has developed a powerful SIS vision is the McKesson Corp., formerly Foremost-McKesson and originally McKesson-Robbins. In 1984, it was the nation's largest independent distributor of:

- *Ethical and proprietary drugs, toiletries, fragrances, and sundries.* These are sold to chain and independent drugstores and hospitals. The company operates over 50 distribution centers, receives more than 50,000 goods from 2,500 suppliers, and serves 14,000 drugstores and 2,000 hospitals in 35 states.
- *Wine and spirits.* These are sold through the company's 36 distribution centers to liquor stores, restaurants, bars, and other establishments. It holds distribution rights from most U.S. distillers, importers, and wineries in one or more markets.

- *Industrial and speciality chemicals.* These are sold through the company's over 60 distribution centers to customers in the pharmaceutical, cosmetic, food, and automobile industries.

McKesson, like D&B, also traces its history back to the first half of the 19th century. Indeed, the growth of independent wholesale jobbers like McKesson-Robbins, Marshall Field, and others was one of the principal reasons for the new type of credit service offered by the Tappans, Duns, and Bradstreets of the day. M–R imported and wholesaled drugs, chemicals, and related lines. By 1926, however, little remained of the original M–R but its name, as competitive pressures and import tariffs forced it to close its distribution business and maintain only a small manufacturing facility in Brooklyn, New York.

Resurrected in the late 20s, M–R at first continued in its traditional lines and then diversified over the next 50 years into such businesses as alcoholic beverage distribution, dairy products (through merger with Foremost Dairies), and pasta and dehydrated vegetable manufacture (through the acquisition of C. F. Mueller Co.). In 1984, the new McKesson announced that it was leaving the food business (having sold Foremost and Muellers in 1983) to concentrate its resources on the value-added distribution of a variety of products.

What is shaping McKesson's new strategic direction is what is shaping D&B's: SIS vision. Top management believes that the name "McKesson Corporation" now "reflects our history, the present structure of our business, and the *path* we are traveling." According to Thomas Drohan, McKesson's former president (now deceased):

> Perhaps the single greatest *advantage* that the McKesson distribution companies enjoy has been—and will continue to be—in *computer technology*, where our size and diversity have enabled us to achieve the necessary critical mass. Our data processing resources now involve 550 people and an annual budget of over $65 million. We intend to continue the proliferation of this technology among our current distribution businesses and to seek out opportunities to

apply it to other distribution-related businesses. This shift in emphasis—making *Value-Added Distribution* our *primary thrust* with a secondary thrust in certain proprietary product areas—reflects the facts as they are today.[3]

McKesson sees a direct connection between its ability to gain competitive advantage and its use of information systems to support and shape strategies aimed at this objective. Over the past 10 years, the company has introduced computer-based goods and services to help it gain an edge with both its suppliers and its customers, an edge that translates into a distinct advantage over other distributors. These strategic moves run the gamut from those designed to exploit scale and scope economies to growth and alliance maneuvers to expand into new markets. Among the SIS and SIS alliances implemented by McKesson, the following are particularly noteworthy:

CosMcK/Econoscan. CosMcK, a computer-based merchandising program created in 1981 for druggists, supermarkets, and mass merchandisers, helps retailers stock, price-label, rotate, and display merchandise according to marketing reports generated by CosMcK. Covering 20 departments in 1982, it now extends to 28 categories such as over-the-counter drugs, pet care, and school supplies.

Econoscan, a computerized order-entry system, enables a retailer holding an Econoscan scanning device to record data from shelf labels and then to transmit the captured data in the form of an order over telephone lines to a McKesson distribution center, at the rate of 600 items per minute. McKesson fills the order overnight and delivers it the next day in tote boxes arranged to correspond to the various shelf divisions of the retailer's store.

What pharmacist Dick Ramsey from Everett, Washington, says about these services indicates their strategic importance to McKesson:

> The people at McKesson have always gone out of their way to encourage success in business, from the CosMcK service merchandisers who manage my various departments—pet supplies, hair and

foot care products, and cosmetics—to their advertising circular program for independent druggists. McKesson has genuinely worked to
help me, as an independent businessman, *survive* in an economic climate where a lot of people don't. . . . We probably save a minimum
of eight man-hours a week that were once spent ordering and putting away merchandise. Now it's as simple as a quick scan of the
shelves with a computerized device that fits right into the palm of
my hand. Time is money, and when I can save time, I know I'm increasing my profits.[4]

McKesson Chemical.   This division, the nation's leading full-
line distributor of industrial chemicals, implemented a computer-
based service for its customers that saves them costly inspection
time and enhances McKesson's image of a high-quality, reliable distributor. At selected chemical distribution centers, McKesson installed highly sensitive instruments to analyze the chemical composition of substances. This ensures, for example, that chemical
solvents meet stringent customer standards. The instruments are
tied via telephone lines to a McKesson computer at its research center in Dublin, California, so that the data can be interpreted and
checked for compliance.

This is another of the many differentiation-based strategic
thrusts supported by McKesson's information systems. McKesson
Chemical, like the drug and alcoholic beverage division, also offers
its customers an on-line order-entry system designed to streamline
ordering, inventory control, purchasing, accounts receivable, delivery, and invoicing procedures. For the chemical division, it provides instantaneous information on inventory, customer needs,
and the safe handling of the more than 1,000 chemical products it
sells. Most likely, economies of scope based on order-entry systems
know-how are at work here.

Pharmaceutical Card System.   PCS, a prescription drug
claims processing system, led McKesson to spin off a special business unit to exploit its potentialities. Introduced a few years ago,
PCS now processes more than 27 million claims from 2.3 million

cardholders covering 6.5 million people. Employers issue PCS cards as an employee benefit. More than 45,000 pharmacies, representing more than 80 percent of the nation's retail druggists, fill prescriptions for PCS cardholders. Coverage is offered by 155 insurance companies in the United States and Canada. Data from pharmacists is transmitted to a central McKesson computer for processing. Claims are completed automatically, and tapes are forwarded to third-party reimbursers.

In itself, PCS represents a strategic diversification maneuver. Perhaps even more interesting is the continued expansion of McKesson's PCS operation, symbolizing the power of the company's SIS vision. As claim data is collected by PCS, a special unit, Pharmaceutical Data Services (PDS), uses its software to analyze the data and produce a series of marketing reports targeted at major drug manufacturers, financial institutions, and government agencies. The reports include analyses of prescription drug use, by hospital, nursing care facility, and the like. It is capable of analyzing the flow of pharmaceutical products through the health care system.

In 1983, PCS acquired Dresden/Davis Organization, a medical research company that collects data on drugs prescribed by physicians. This, of course, will become part of PCS's growing data base and move the unit closer to its goal of "becoming a full-service market research company and the nation's leading supplier of health care data."

Acquisition of SKU. In 1983, McKesson joined Action Industries Inc., a Pittsburgh maker of household and hardware items, in a 50–50 venture in which they acquired SKU Inc., a microcomputer software distributor. The leader in the embryonic micro software industry at the time was Softsel Computer Products (1983 sales estimate, $75 million), followed by Micro D (1983 sales estimate, $28 million), and SKU (1983 sales estimate, $25 million). The market for personal computer software, then at $2.1 billion, was projected to reach $11.7 billion by 1988, with 25 percent handled by independent distributors. It is "the nation's fastest growing distribution business," the president and chief executive officer of McKesson Corporation claimed in 1983.

Whatever Action's motives, McKesson's aim was clear: to expand the scope of its distribution business and transform the cottage industry of software distribution (with aftertax margins of 4 percent at most) into a larger, more profitable game. McKesson planned to use previously developed information systems as the synergistic fuel for its entry vehicle. The computerized order-entry systems and other proprietary products it provides to over 14,000 mass merchandisers, supermarkets, and other outlets, would be tailored to this new marketplace. These information systems would not be used merely as aids to improve efficiency but as weapons to shape competitive strategy.

"The name of the game," McKesson's CEO said at the time, "has become adding value to distribution. Our primary goal is to set ourselves apart from the competition in dramatic enough ways that we become the first distributor a supplier thinks of. At the other end, by tying your customers to you as tightly as possible, you get more and more of his business as he grows."

With the past as prologue to the future, current and new participants in the software distribution industry could expect McKesson to use its information systems to gain competitive advantage by:

- Establishing on-line links with software suppliers and retailers.
- Providing information to suppliers and retailers to help them better manage inventories, collect and analyze market data, and plan sales campaigns.
- Providing retailers with shelf management plans, price labels, inventory systems, etc.
- Conducting computer-related technical seminars for suppliers and retailers.
- Joining with software suppliers to develop new products.
- Marketing associated services through its network.

Unfortunately for McKesson and Action, however, this strategic alliance failed. In August 1984, the partners announced they were writing off their combined investment of $8 million and discontinuing the operations of SKU. A spokesman for McKesson said that "the market for computer software hasn't developed as we had anticipated." The parties were unable to stem accelerating losses at SKU.

I include this example of a failed strategic thrust to emphasize the point that strategic moves entail considerable risks, and neither information systems support nor shaping nor anything else can guarantee success with certainty. What looked like a promising move failed because market demand was misread.

While this venture failed, another seems headed for success. In 1983, McKesson purchased 3 P.M., a software developer and marketer of packages for pharmacies and florists. In 1984, McKesson negotiated a pact with the Florists' Transworld Delivery Association. Under the terms of the agreement, McKesson will deliver, install, and maintain personal computers and systems intended to handle a florist's business management functions like payroll and accounts receivable and payable. It expects sales from this new venture to total about $75 million over the next five-year period.

Banc One

The final example of a successfully developed SIS vision involves one of the most innovative and entrepreneurial firms in the financial services industry, Banc One of Columbus, Ohio. John G. McCoy, the chief executive officer of this multibank-holding company formed in 1967, retired in 1984 at age 71 after 25 years in that position. When he took the reins at City National Bank (Banc One's forerunner) from his father in 1959, the bank had under $150 million in assets and primarily business customers.

With assets of over $7 billion and customers drawn primarily from the consumer sector, Banc One ranked in 1984 in the top 10 among the 100 largest banks in the United States on three commonly acknowledged measures of superior performance. Through an ongoing series of mergers, it now controls 22 affiliate banks in Ohio. For the 16th consecutive year, net income and earnings per share have increased. In the 1980–83 period, net income skyrocketed from

$32.8 million to $83.3 million, employees from 3,145 to 6,939, and branch offices from 127 to 314.

These figures represent an extraordinary record of profitability and growth. How can it be explained? Why has Banc One, a relatively small, local bank in 1967, been able to succeed so well in the increasingly competitive financial services industry, where the competition consists not only of banking colossi like Citibank, Chase, and Chemical but also of retail giants like Sears and financial supermarkets like American Express?

While a number of explanations running from luck to charisma have been suggested, I believe that the most convincing account of Banc One's success can be given in terms of its powerful SIS vision— a vision embodied, to be sure, in McCoy, but a vision nevertheless of the integral role to be played by information systems in the bank's strategic evolution.

McCoy, like some of his colleagues, long believed that banks competed at a disadvantage vis-à-vis such omnibus rivals as Sears or American Express. While the latter were free to develop an almost unlimited product portfolio or expand without geographical limit, banks were handcuffed in these two strategic areas by federal and state regulations. Unless banks could find ways around the regulations or get them changed in their favor, they faced the growing prospect of erosion in some of their major business lines.

McCoy's strategic response to these threats was twofold. First, to overcome the geographical expansion constraint, he formed the Banc One holding company, which permitted the acquisition of other banks but not across state lines. Second, to overcome the product development restriction, he encouraged his managers to search for new products that would yield new sources of income and would protect the bank's cash flow stream from exposure to interest-rate fluctuations. Thus, expansion through acquisition and product innovation were two strategic thrusts that Banc One would follow in its strategic journey. Both, it turned out, were precisely the kinds of thrusts that could be supported or shaped by information systems.

McCoy developed his SIS vision early. When he assumed the presidency, one of his first moves was to seek board approval for an annual R&D budget, not to exceed 3 percent of annual profits. He won approval, and every year, Banc One has been able to experiment, primarily in the area of information systems. In 1966, for example, it introduced the first Bank Americard credit card service outside California. In 1967, it initiated a major on-line credit card processing network that today spans over 30 states. In 1971, it joined with IBM in making the first significant test of point-of-sale systems using magnetically encoded cards. In 1980, with others, it conducted the first test of in-home banking through the use of customer TVs and the telephone system.

From the 60s, McCoy realized the importance of information systems in the financial services industry. In a recent interview, he was asked why Banc One was so eager to become the first Bank of America licensee, and what made him think it was such a good idea.

> Well, there was some luck involved but you have to remember that was the time when the computer was first beginning to produce important changes in banking. We thought the credit card was an idea whose time had come because of the new computer capability. The first on-line computer systems in banking were designed for credit card authorization. We had one of the first ones here in Columbus. *We committed major efforts to computer development in those early years and we still do today*, I might add. By 1970, to tell you how this *innovation* happens, we began to install the first automatic teller machine equipment in our Upper Arlington branch because we saw it as a way to link the customer, with a plastic card, directly to the computer. [Italics added.][5]

As Banc One's reputation for information system innovation grew, other firms approached it for processing services. In the late 70s, Merrill Lynch contracted with Banc One for data processing and Visa debit card issuance services associated with its new Cash Management Account (CMA). As a result of this SIS alliance, now also negotiated with other brokerage houses, Banc One is one of the nation's three largest Visa processors.

The primary vehicle to expand Banc One's processing services— related chiefly to credit and debit card processing outside Ohio banking markets, and producing more than 30 percent of the corporation's net income—is the Financial Card Services Division. This spinoff has had an impressive growth record.

> In 1983 the cardholder account base processed by Financial Card Services grew by 41.3 percent to over 3.9 million. Of these accounts, 14 percent are Banc One affiliate banks' customers and 7 percent are Banc One customers originating from outside our market area, while 79 percent are derived from third-party processing for other banks, thrifts, credit unions, finance companies, and brokers. Financial Card Services revenue grew 26 percent in 1983. This resulted from growth in Banc One customer accounts and in third-party processing contracts originated within the last several years. The relatively more mature Merrill Lynch processing program generated a 4 percent revenue increase in 1983.
>
> Late in 1983 a new four-year contract was negotiated with Merrill Lynch relating to Banc One's processing of its "CMA" brokerage accounts. This is the third contract Banc One has had with Merrill Lynch since 1977 when Banc One was selected to be the processor for this revolutionary financial product. Although this contract permits Merrill Lynch the option of converting to internal processing of the CMA debit cards, Banc One will receive consulting fees from Merrill Lynch for assisting in this conversion over several years. Management contemplates this contract will produce more revenues to Banc One than the previous three-year contracts combined.[6]

While credit and debit card processing is important to Banc One's overall strategic scheme, it is the centralization of bank processing activities that has enabled the holding company to make its acquisition program work.

A small bank sees in the Banc One affiliation (read: acquisition) proposition an opportunity to cope with the accelerating changes in financial services that would otherwise engulf it—new regulations, the prospect of interstate banking, interest-rate deregulation, and perhaps the most critical, new technology demands induced by the convergence of information processing and telecommunications.

For Banc One, its acquisition program—called the "Uncommon Partnership" because it allows the acquired bank a reasonable degree of independence—enables it to reap large economies of scale. Listen to McCoy on this partnership:

> More recently the "Uncommon Partnership" represents our chosen way of managing the holding company even though we could merge everything into a single bank. Instead, each bank is run by bankers from that area; each trying to be sensitive to community needs. As a result, a lot of our management strength and certainly the growth and earnings potential, lies with our affiliates. *We have limited the concentration of management to those areas that are most sensitive to economies of scale such as data processing* or the handling of investments. I expect this philosophy will remain for some time into the future. [Italics added.]⁷

Thus, Banc One uses the strategic cost thrust to shape its competitive strategy of growth via acquisition. In the case of a recent affiliation, according to another officer at Banc One, "We were able to save almost a million dollars a year in combined operating expenses by converting the affiliates' data processing systems into our single system. There are some real economies of scale at work here."

Banc One also forged an innovative strategic alliance with Comp–U–Card, a computerized shopping and below-retail buying service. The two partners created Super Visa, a credit card issued by Banc One that CUC offered as bait to lure new customers. The card carries a $1,000 line of credit and can be used to buy consumer goods (watches, washing machines, and the like) through CUC. Under the terms of the agreement between Banc One and CUC, customers pay an annual fee of $25 for the card and the shopping service package. This is split 50–50 between the two partners. On purchases that roll over, Banc One assesses a 21.6 percent annual rate.

This SIS alliance serves CUC's purpose of enhancing its offering to customers and forgoing the risk and expense associated with starting its own credit card system. For Banc One, the alliance has already increased the bank's credit card account base by 100 percent. This has proved to be particularly profitable, as CUC's customers have tended to let their accounts roll over to a greater extent than Banc One's other cardholders.

For Dun & Bradstreet, McKesson, and Banc One, SIS vision functions as a creative force transforming the organization through strategic moves supported or shaped by information systems. Other organizations such as Citibank, Federal Express, McDonnell Douglas, American Hospital Supply, and GE (discussed in the chapters to follow) also possess SIS vision. Each comprehends, in its fashion, the strategic importance of information systems.

SIS vision is an ability that can be developed and hence possessed in varying degrees. Its most important prerequisite is the adoption of the strategic perspective on information systems. Absent this, the systematic search and exploitation of SIS opportunities would be doomed. The conventional perspective countenances the existence of only two information system varieties: MIS and MSS. Like the Western astronomers blinded by their religious beliefs to the existence of a vast array of planetary phenomena, firms in the thrall of the conventional perspective lack the vision to see the cornucopia of SIS opportunities falling forever beyond their line of sight.

But by adopting the strategic perspective on information systems, by donning a new pair of conceptual glasses, the world of SIS opportunities appears. It is the aim of this brief book to sketch the strategic perspective and to provide the lenses organizations can use to guide their SIS planning and implementation efforts.

CASE REFERENCES

Action Industries   See McKesson.

American Air   *American Way*, September 1984; *Business Week*, August 23, 1982; May 23, 1983; May 7, 1984; *New York Times*, April 29, 1984.

Banc One   *ABA Banking Journal*, December 1983; *Bankers Magazine*, September–October 1981; *The Wall Street Journal*, September 11, 1984; annual reports, 1979–83.

Dun & Bradstreet   *Computerworld*, November 21, 1983; *Information Systems News*, September 15, 1983; November 14, 1983; June 18, 1984; *Management Technology*, July 1984; *New York Times*, May 21, 1984; September 20, 1984; *Software News*, November 1983; *The Wall Street Journal*, May 9, 1984; May 18, 1984; annual reports, 1979–83.

IBM   See International MarketNet.

International MarketNet   *Business Week*, April 2, 1984; *Information Systems News*, September 10, 1984; *New York Times*, March 22, 1984; *The Wall Street Journal*, March 22, 1984; May 17, 1984.

McKesson   *Business Week*, December 7, 1981; *Drug Topics*, June 20, 1983; *New York Times*, December 14, 1983; August 26, 1984; October 14, 1984; *The Wall Street Journal*, October 24, 1983; January 6, 1984; April 6, 1984; July 23, 1984; Annual Report, 1983.

Merrill Lynch   See International MarketNet.

Metpath   *Business Week*, January 25, 1982; *New York Times*, July 21, 1984.

Monchik-Weber   See International MarketNet.

Paine Webber   *The Wall Street Journal*, December 23, 1983; February 15, 1984; April 1, 1984.

State Street Bank & Trust   See **Paine Webber.**

United Air   See **American Air.**

BIBLIOGRAPHY

Anthony, Robert N. *Planning and Control Systems: A Framework for Analysis.* Cambridge, Mass.: Harvard University Press, 1965.

Chandler, Alfred D., Jr. *The Visible Hand: The Managerial Revolution in American Business.* Cambridge, Mass.: Harvard University Press, 1977.

Kuhn, Thomas S. *The Structure of Scientific Revolutions.* 2d ed. Chicago: University of Chicago Press, 1970.

Nolan, Richard L. "The Plight of the EDP Manager." *Harvard Business Review*, May–June 1973.

Wohl, Stanley. *The Medical Industrial Complex.* New York: Crown Publishers, 1984.

Zani, William. "Blueprint for MIS." *Harvard Business Review*, November–December 1970.

2

Strategic Perspective

STRATEGIC THRUSTS AT GENERAL MOTORS

The strategic perspective on information systems finds its conceptual support in an analytical framework that attempts to capture the major moves open to organizations in search of advantage. I call this framework the *theory of strategic thrusts*. By supporting or shaping the organization's strategic thrusts, SIS support or shape its competitive strategy. Strategic thrusts therefore constitute the critical interface linking competitive strategy and information systems.

Before characterizing the theory and showing how it relates directly to well-known works in the strategy field, we need first to review some samples of strategic thrusts made in the course of an organization's evolution. These will reveal the range of opportunities open to the firm seeking advantage.

The history of American industry is replete with just these kinds of major moves that have resulted in a competitive edge: vertical integration along an industry chain, innovation in product or process, diversification or entry into related businesses, economies of scale, product differentiation, and acquisitions or other alliances. Each is illustrated in the classic chronicle of William Durant, the founder of General Motors, and by some of GM's actions under Alfred Sloan, Durant's successor, in the embryonic and growth stages of the automotive industry.

Prior to forming GM in 1908, Durant was in the carriage business, having created in 1885 the Durant-Dort Carriage Company with Dallas Dort, a hardware salesman. Durant-Dort began with neither manufacturing facilities nor a distribution network. To stimulate business for their product, a new kind of cart, the partners first had to persuade dealers and distributors to promote it. When orders wheeled in, they contracted with a local manufacturer to produce the carts.

As demand accelerated, Durant-Dort expanded by building its own assembly plant. This strategic move helped reduce costs, putting the company in a better position relative to its direct competitors—other carriage manufacturers. But when demand increased still further, the firm found itself caught in the classic double bind of losing sales to competitors, and hence market share, and paying premium prices to suppliers who were acting opportunistically toward it. To secure control over the supplier bottleneck and to cut costs, costs that put it at a competitive disadvantage vis-à-vis its suppliers *and* its direct competitors, Durant-Dort decided to internalize these transactions, this time setting up or financing specialty plants to produce parts needed in its assembly works. From the *assembly* of carts and carriages, Durant-Dort had again expanded its operations to include the *manufacture* of bodies, wheels, axles, upholstery, and springs. Expansion enabled it to gain advantage by reducing the edge enjoyed by its suppliers and direct competitors.

Following backward integration, Durant-Dort grew again via moves that extended its product line. By 1900, its factories were manufacturing a full array of carriages, carts, wagons, buggies, etc., all sold under the Blue Ribbon trademark. Just 15 years after the founding of Durant-Dort, Durant's entrepreneurial acumen had made him a millionaire.

But even though the company became the leading wagon and carriage producer in the United States, its prospects were far from bright. Whatever competitive advantage Durant-Dort may have attained in its marketplace—being the low-cost producer or the manufacturer of the most highly differentiated product inducing the greatest customer loyalty—would be rendered worthless if a new product, the horseless carriage, caught on. Remember, this was the turn of the century, when the automobile industry was moving only in first gear. In 1900, the United States produced fewer than 5,000 cars. In 1902, 12 firms manufactured automobiles; one year later the total climbed to 24. The next year, 12 new entrants sprouted. In 1903, the leading manufacturer was Ransom Olds, whose Oldsmobile held 25 percent of the market; 10 years later, Ford produced 182,000 Model Ts, winning 39.4 percent of the expanding automobile market. In 1904, Durant entered the embryonic industry by acquiring the assets of the Buick Motor Company, a bankrupt automobile manufacturer.

This strategic move—prompted by the automobile's threat to carriagemakers as a substitute mode of transportation, by the availability of related managerial and other resources at Durant-

Dort, and by Durant's entrepreneurial vision and empire-building talents—led in four years to the formation of General Motors. The steps Durant took with Buick reflected the moves he had made previously with Durant-Dort and presaged those he would take as the head of GM.

He redesigned the Buick, built large assembly plants, and established a national marketing and sales network by granting franchises in rural areas to regional distributors (who would be responsible for managing local dealers) and by opening retail outlets to sell directly to consumers in large cities. In both manufacturing and selling, Durant relied on the underutilized, slack managerial and technical talents drawn from his carriage business. Charles Nash, for example, the production manager of the carriageworks, became head of the Buick company. As the volume of sales orders increased, Durant again initiated an expansion program, integrating backward to cut transaction costs and avoid supply bottlenecks. It acquired in the process, for example, Weston-Mott and Champion, the former a manufacturer of axles and wheels, the latter of sparkplugs. As a result of such acquisitions and other strategic moves, Buick became the leading automobile manufacturer in the United States, increasing its production from 31 cars in 1904 to 8,487 in 1908, with Ford in second place with 6,181 and Cadillac third with 2,380.

Predicting sales of over a million cars a year and with the lessons learned at Durant-Dort and Buick imprinted on his mind, Durant concluded in 1908 that the best way to meet this anticipated, unprecedented demand was to grow by forming alliances. Rejected by Ford and Olds, the founders of two other car manufacturers, Durant formed the GM holding company, which, in its first two years, obtained complete or partial control of Buick, Olds, Cadillac, 8 other automobile companies, 2 electrical lamp companies, and 12 auto and accessory manufacturers.

But Durant's predictions proved erroneous, forcing his resignation from the presidency of GM in 1910. He was replaced by Storrow, who (with the support of GM's bankers) introduced administrative changes aimed at improving efficiency by consolidating joint activities like purchasing, accounting, and engineering.

Durant, however, was not to be denied. In the years following his resignation, he took control of Chevrolet, an integrated, high-volume automobile company, and developed important financial ties with members of the Du Pont family. Parlaying these resources, he regained control of GM in 1916. Another round of supplier acquisitions followed, among them the Hyatt Roller Bearing Company, which brought with it Alfred Sloan, the organizational wizard who succeeded Durant.

To pave the road for increased sales, GM introduced a radically new vehicle in 1919, the GM Acceptance Corporation. This financial innovation revolutionized the automotive credit business. Prior to the formation of GMAC, dealers, distributors, and consumers had no reliable source of credit for their automobile purchases, as banks seemed to have "a moral objection to financing a luxury, believing apparently whatever fostered consumption must discourage thrift. Consequently, automobiles were sold to consumers mainly for cash." Dealers and distributors also frequently lacked funds to finance inventories and retail installment sales; local banks were simply too rigid to meet the demand generated by the mass production of automobiles. The GMAC innovation gave GM an advantage in its struggles with other automobile manufacturers and in bargaining negotiations with its distributors and dealers. These latter complained that GM forced them to finance exclusively through GMAC; in 1939, the U.S. government initiated criminal proceedings against GM on this matter. The court found GM guilty. But it was not until 1952, after a long battle with the Antitrust Division of the Justice Department, that GM consented to change the ground rules under which it and its distributors and dealers operated.

GM's moves to alter business practices and thereby establish competitive advantage were not, of course, limited to the financial area. External competitive threats and internal management crises prompted innovations in organization and product policy that had equally profound effects on the automobile industry. As a result of these strategic moves, GM upset the competitive balance in the industry, securing for itself (at least among its domestic competitors) what has proved to be an insurmountable advantage.

In the first years of the 20s, GM viewed the Ford Motor Company as its principal external threat. Under the aegis of its founder, Henry Ford, the company had won the top spot in the growing industry, climbing from a 9.7 percent share of the market in 1909 to 55.7 percent in 1921. These figures count only sales for the Ford Model T, first offered in 1908 and essentially unchanged for 19 years thereafter.

Ford, less interested in design innovation than in production advances, pioneered the application of assembly-line operations in the automotive industry, with its concommitant standardization and specialization of manufacturing processes and labor efforts. His goal was to provide the most inexpensive, reliable car to the greatest number of consumers at the least cost. In this, he succeeded admirably. In 1909, the price of the Model T touring car was $950 (12,000 sold); in 1913, $550 (182,000 sold); in 1917, $450 (741,000 sold); in 1921, the height of Ford's supremacy, $355 (845,000 sold). The Spartan Ford firm ran a lean, mean operation. It presented a formidable opponent to the Athenian GM, an organization composed of far too many quasi-independent, free thinking units, each tooting its own horn. This was the challenge Sloan faced when he took the wheel in 1923. At the time of his ascendancy, GM's market share was 20 percent, essentially unchanged from where it was in 1910 under Durant. By 1929, GM had replaced Ford as the industry leader, capturing 32.3 percent of new car sales to Ford's 31.3 percent; in 1933, the margin widened: 41.4 percent to 20.7 percent. What, then, did GM do under Sloan to gain such a competitive advantage?

Two related innovations were critical. The first dealt with GM's internal management crisis, the second with Ford and the other car manufacturers. GM suffered, Sloan argued, from excessive decentralization as a result of its policy of rapid expansion and acquisition following World War I. The remedy, Sloan concluded, was greater coordination and integration of activities. Without such, top management would never know or prove "where the efficiencies and inefficiencies lay, there being no objective basis for the allocation of new investment." Fundamental to Sloan's view on management problems was his belief that the strategic aim of any business should be to earn a satisfactory return on capital. If not achieved, management must correct the deficiency or dispose of the activity for a more profitable one. Without improved coordination and integration, Sloan contended, GM would never be in a position to make rational decisions about such matters and so would never be able to compete head to head with Ford.

Through Sloan's efforts, GM became one of the first businesses in the United States to adopt the multidivisional form of organization. This structure gave GM self-contained divisions (e.g., Chevrolet, Buick, and Cadillac), each having its own engineering, production, and sales functions and an array of corporate staff groups (e.g., R&D, finance) to coordinate and support the activities of the divisions. At the top of the managerial hierarchy, to resolve divisional conflicts and to set corporate policy, was the executive committee.

Prior to the new structure, each unit acted independently, setting its own prices and production rules (which often placed some GM cars in direct competition with others) with no regard for the general wellbeing of GM. Under Sloan's regime, pricing and product policy became a matter for the executive committee to decide. Through this organizational innovation, GM had taken the first step toward upsetting the competitive balance.

According to Sloan, "the fundamental conception of the *advantage* to be secured in this business was expressed by cooperation and coordination of our various policies and divisions." Sloan and his colleagues thus rejected the notion that it was essential that GM's production, advertising, selling, or servicing activities for any particular product be more efficient than its best competitor. For it was assumed that greater efficiency would be achieved through divisional cooperation and coordination, once the GM units stopped working at cross-purposes.

Sloan's second strategic move transformed GM's laissez-faire product line policy into a powerful competitive weapon. Where Ford had achieved domination and low-cost producer status through almost fanatical dedication to the production of essentially one product, the Model T, GM sought its competitive advantage through a policy of product differentiation. Sloan's administration formulated a strategy that called for the production of six standard models, distinguished by well-defined price, quality, design, and other features. Each car in the GM product line would now be integral, conceived in relation to other models in the line, with Chevrolet at the bottom and Cadillac at the top—the price range of Cadillac being set at about six times that of Chevrolet.

Sloan was crystal clear about the new product policy and its aim of mass-producing a full line of cars graded upward in quality and price. "This principle supplied the first element in *differentiating* the General Motor's concept of the market from that of the old, Ford Model T concept." The new policy put GM's Chevrolet in direct competition, for the first time, with the Model T.

The strategic move toward product differentiation, coupled with Sloan's multidivisional structural innovation, catapulted GM, within a decade, to the leadership role it has held since that time. The automobile industry is not, as Ford viewed it, a commodity business. Manufacturers take great pains to differentiate their products from those of their rivals, through design, advertising, and the like. They aim to establish long-lasting brand loyalties, for repeat buying is a vital part of the car market. Sloan and GM were the first to realize these truths and to capitalize on them. Through such moves, GM established the competitive edge it has maintained for the past 50 years.

We conclude our discussion of the Durant-GM-Sloan annals with some strategic moves of another sort: growth via diversification thrusts into nonautomotive markets. Success in diversification often depends on a firm's ability to transfer skills and resources from existing activities to the new venture. For GM, such transfers involved mass-production engineering know-how and the management expertise accompanying it.

According to Sloan, GM "never made anything except 'durable products,' and they have always, with minor exceptions, been connected with motors. Not even Mr. Durant, for all his expansion and diversification, ever suggested that we should stray into any field clearly outside the boundary suggested by our corporate name,

General Motors." GM's interest in diversification seems to have been primarily defensive, either as a hedge against the vagaries of automobile demand or the threat of substitute products that might replace the automobile. But in some situations, GM recognized a growth opportunity and entered the business to exploit it. In any case, Sloan states, "we never had a master plan for nonautomotive ventures; we got into them for different reasons, and we were very lucky at some critical points."

GM entered the diesel business in the early 30s, at the time when the dominant engine driving the locomotive industry was designed for steam. Prior to GM's entry, locomotives had always been built to a railroad's custom specifications, so that no two in the United States were alike. GM changed this, not through technological innovation, but by the transfer of its manufacturing, engineering, and marketing know-how from the automotive arena to the locomotive. GM manufactured *standardized* diesel locomotives produced in volume, guaranteed to perform at a lower cost per ton mile than steam-driven ones, and maintained by a dedicated service organization, using standard replacement parts. In less than a decade, GM's diesels outsold all other locomotive producers combined. By capitalizing on its own underutilized management and technical resources, GM won the competitive battle. Through this diversification move, it became the dominant producer in a new industry, selling new products in new markets.

In 1918, GM bought the near-bankrupt firm, Guardian Refrigerator Corporation. After considerable effort by engineers at the GM R&D labs and a name change, the "new" Frigidaire became the market leader in less than a decade. GM stated in its 1925 *Annual Report*:

> This apparatus lends itself both from the standpoint of type of manufacture as well as market possibilities to quantity production. The Corporation believes that through its broad experience in quality manufacture, its research activities and through its purchasing ability on account of the large volume of its operations, it can more than maintain the dominating position that Frigidaire now enjoys.[8]

By 1933, GM's Frigidaire Division itself adopted a diversification strategy by increasing the depth of its air-conditioning line, offering units for all fields of application—home, office, hotel, hospital, etc.; in 1936, it increased the width of its product line by moving into electric ranges and other household accessories and equipment.

In 1928, fearing the possibility that personal airplanes might someday replace cars, GM diversified again, this time into the aircraft industry, purchasing a 40 percent stake in the Fokker Aircraft Corporation of America and a 20 percent interest in the newly formed Bendix Aviation Corporation. A short time later, it acquired a 30 percent share of North American Aviation, a company that once controlled both TWA and Eastern airlines.

GM, it seems, was anxious about the possibility of a small plane being produced for everyday family use, a development that Sloan believed would entail, to say the least, large unforeseeable consequences for the automobile industry. To be protected, GM declared itself in the aviation industry. It "felt that, in view of the more or less close relationship in an engineering way between the airplane and the motor car, its operating organization, technical and otherwise, should be placed in a position where it would have an opportunity to come into contact with the particular problems involved in transportation by air." As it turned out, the threat never materialized, and GM made less of an impact through its engineering genius than through the management expertise it provided to Fokker, Bendix, and North American.

Sloan, in fact, believed that this was perhaps GM's greatest contribution to the airline industry. Through its board memberships and managerial contacts with these aerospace companies, GM was able to transfer some of its managerial skills to its investments. This most likely helped these firms compete more effectively and build commanding positions in their respective segments of the aviation industry.

As they grew, so did the value of GM's investment in them. When, in the late 40s, GM decided to liquidate its aviation holdings, it did so only to release capital to fuel its automotive operations, which after World War II were growing rapidly.

THE THEORY OF STRATEGIC THRUSTS

Over the evolutionary span just sketched, GM made major moves related to product differentiation, cost reduction, product line expansion, diversification, vertical integration, and acquisition. These and hundreds of similar moves undertaken by other enterprises reflect a somewhat daunting multiplicity of strategic actions. The theory of strategic thrusts is intended to simplify this multiplicity by reducing it to five generic strategic thrusts. I call these thrusts *differentiation, cost, innovation, growth,* and *alliance.* It is my contention that these are adequate to account for most of the major moves organizations make in search of advantage.

Relying for a moment on the everyday meaning of these thrusts (each will be described more fully in the next five chapters, when I show how information systems can be used to support or shape them), let us examine some of their properties.

First, they manifest *strategic polarities*. By this I mean that they are capable of assuming opposing sets of attributes, depending upon their strategic use. When GM formulated its product policy under Sloan, it was using differentiation *offensively* to gain competitive advantage. Another company might use this move *defensively* by taking steps to reduce the differentiation advantage of its rivals and thereby advance its own competitive position (see the Honeywell Building Controls Group example in Chapter 3).

Reducing costs and becoming the low-cost producer in an industry often leads to competitive advantage. But a company that can manipulate factors that will *raise* the costs of its competitors may also establish a competitive edge by this maneuver. Alternatively, helping suppliers or customers *decrease* their costs may win the approval of these stakeholders and ultimately serve as an important competitive advantage in battles against direct rivals. Cost may be used *offensively* when a company attempts to reduce its supplier costs so that it can better compete by reducing its prices vis-à-vis its direct competitors. Cost may also be used *defensively* by organizations that are attempting to reduce the leverage vendors or customers may have over them.

An innovation in production, processing, or product quality may *increase* the competitive advantage an organization currently enjoys, while another may serve to *decrease* the edge rivals may have. Some may use innovation *offensively* to preempt, while others may use it *defensively* to imitate.

Growth via volume or geographical expansion, backward or forward integration, product line or entry diversification, may succeed in *increasing* competitive advantage and hence be an *offensive* weapon in an organization's arsenal, or it may be used as a *defensive* weapon aimed at *reducing* the opportunities of rivals to gain an edge.

Alliances—joint ventures, acquisitions, and the like—may be arranged to support or shape differentiation, cost, innovation, or growth moves. Hence, they too exhibit the strategic polarities just mentioned.

Second, members of this generic set of strategic moves frequently occur in combination. To gain competitive edge, for instance, a growth-via-backward-integration maneuver, intended primarily to internalize market transactions, may also be aimed at reducing costs (and prices) through an innovative use of technology, made possible by the combining of acquired and existing resources.

Third, members of this set are subject to a variety of ordering or degree relations. For example, a cost reduction may be major, medium, or minor and a differentiation, innovation, alliance, or growth move may be short-term or long-term.

Fourth, members of this set are often related by dialectical processes such as the one illustrated above by Durant's jump from carriages into automobiles. Recall that Durant-Dort had evolved into the leading carriage and wagon producer in the United States. To be in that position, it had either a cost or a differentiation advantage. Yet, Durant knew that this edge would be worthless if the automobile replaced the carriage as the primary mode of household transportation. In terms of strategic options, therefore, innovation, growth via diversification, or alliance were open to him as possible moves to transform the nature of Durant-Dort's activities so that it could survive in the new automotive environment. But innovation in the carriage industry wouldn't be worth the effort, assuming Durant's hypothesis. Therefore, he had only two options, and to build his new enterprise he pursued both: growth via diversification (making use of resources drawn from Durant-Dort) and alliance formation.

When Durant's empire-building activities came to a close and Sloan was left to rationalize GM's uncoordinated holdings, the dialectical process culminated (temporarily at least) as the focal points of competitive advantage switched from growth and alliance to cost, differentiation, and innovation maneuvers; when these were exhausted, the dialectic resumed again with the pursuit of growth or alliance opportunities.

I call the set of generic moves exhibiting the above four properties *strategic thrusts*. By extension, I use this term to refer to the members of this set, to an organization's strategic differentiation, cost, innovation, growth, and alliance moves, and to associated concepts, leaving context as the final arbiter of meaning.

The notion of strategic thrusts sketched above is linked directly to two important works on strategy: Alfred Chandler's *Strategy and Structure: Chapters in the History of American Industrial Enterprise* (1962) and Michael Porter's *Competitive Strategy: Techniques for Analyzing Industries and Competitors* (1980). Chandler's research on the relationship between an enterprise's growth strategy and the organizational form adopted to execute it led to the rapid expansion of the business strategy field in the 60s and 70s. It was the point of departure for the most influential strategic thinkers of that period (Igor Ansoff, George Steiner, Kenneth Andrews, Seymour Tilles, and others). Porter's application of concepts developed by Joe Bain, and other industrial organization economists, to the competitive strategy area in the later 70s and early 80s has sparked another expansion of the field as researchers and practitioners rush to explore the ramifications of his work.

If, as Chandler suggests, a growth strategy involves "the determination of the basic long-term goals and objectives of the organization," and if "decisions to expand the volume of activities, to set up distant plants and offices, to move into new economic functions, or become diversified along many lines of business" are among the most important strategic decisions an organization can make, then strategic thrusts are those actions associated with such decisions. The strategic thrusts of growth (through expansion, vertical integration, and diversification) and alliance formation (through mergers, acquisitions, and other combinations) are ipso facto tied closely to an organization's growth strategy.

As a result of his studies on the relation between strategy and structure, Chandler hypothesized a pattern of growth and development followed, in varying degrees, by the largest firms in the United States. During Stage 1 in Chandler's growth model, the single-product (-function, -plant, -office, -location, -industry) firm might pursue a growth-via-volume-expansion strategy in response to accelerating demand for its product. This might entail increasing the scale of its sales, manufacturing, or distribution operations, depending on the firm's primary function. It might also, concurrently or sequentially, follow a growth-via-geographical-expansion strategy, establishing units in different parts of the country. As its scale grew, the firm might decide to participate in other functions along its industry chain, from supplying raw materials to retail distribution. It would therefore adopt a growth-via-backward- (or forward-) integration (usually through acquisition) strategy, depending on the opportunities open to it.

The emergence of the huge, vertically integrated firm marked, for Chandler, the end of Stage 1 and the start of Stage 2. It should be clear to the reader that each strategic move made during Stage 1 is an instance of either strategic growth or alliance thrusts. The formation of the firm itself might have been due to a new product or a fundamental change in the method of conducting business in an industry. If so, these would be instances of the strategic innovation thrust.

In Stage 2, the sprawling empires developed strategies to reduce unit costs, enhance product quality and services in response to competitive offerings, improve inefficiently coordinated activities among its functional groups, and so on. Technology often played a critical role during this stage, with such firms as Swift (a gigantic, nationwide distribution and marketing organization in the meat-packing industry at the turn of the century) the first to move innovatively in the application of the new telephone and telegraph services. These telecommunication technologies enabled Swift to coordinate the activities of its stockyards, packing plants, district offices (which operated warehouses and controlled wholesale, and often retail, outlets), and corporate headquarters. Swift substantially reduced costly errors due to misallocation of supply and demand. Again, the strategic actions taken during Stage 2, like those made in Stage 1, are instances of strategic thrusts: differentiation, cost, and innovation.

The successful Stage 2 firms established significant and, in some cases, long-lasting competitive advantages. But they couldn't prevent competitors from emulating their efforts and thereby eroding these advantages. There are limits on the efficiencies to be obtained in purchasing, production, distribution, marketing, etc. As the differences between enterprises receded, profit margins dropped.

> More intensive advertising, product differentiation and improvement, and similar strategies might increase one firm's share of the market, but only major changes in technology, population, and national income could expand the overall market for a single line of products. As the market became more saturated and the opportunities to cut costs through more rational techniques lessened, enterprises began to search for other markets or to develop other businesses that might profitably employ some of their partially utilized resources or even make a more profitable application of those still being fully employed.[9]

For Chandler, this situation signaled the onset of Stage 3: continued growth, essentially reached through diversification. Firms offering a single line might follow a growth-via-full-line-diversification strategy, thus making a range of comparable products available to their customers. In Stage 3, meat packers would diversify into eggs, poultry, and dairy products, taking advantage of economies of scope made possible by excess refrigeration capacity in their distribution network. Others might diversify into international markets. Still others might grow by finding new uses for old products, by developing by-products, by transferring to other areas resources dedicated to one product line or industry, and so on. According to Chandler, "the enterprises whose resources were the most transferable remained those whose men and equipment came to handle a range of technology, rather than a set of end products." Among these were firms involved in the chemical, electrical and electronic, and power machinery industries—industries that also invested the largest percentages of their resources in research and development projects.

Just as Stage 1 (accumulating resources) closed with the need to coordinate inefficiently run operations and led to Stage 2 (rationalizing the use of resources), Stage 3 (continued growth) produced inefficiencies that called for action. It came in Stage 4: rationalizing the use of expanding resources. Organizational innovations—like Sloan's introduction of the multidivisional structure to handle GM's semiautonomous, diverse operations, and the institutionalization of the strategy of diversification—are this stage's most important features of interest to us.

Other researchers (among them Scott, Rumelt, and Galbraith) have improved Chandler's model by refining his analysis of the stages of growth and the strategy of diversification. We need not dwell on these. Suffice it to say these articulations of Chandler's ideas do not affect the main point being made here: Strategic thrusts are fundamentally involved in each stage of a firm's evolution. This fact must be kept in mind by those adopting the strategic perspective on information systems.

For Porter, competitive strategy involves "taking offensive or defensive actions to create a defendable position in an industry, to cope successfully with the five competitive forces [i.e., threat of entry, intensity of rivalry among existing firms, pressures from substitute products, bargaining power of buyers, and bargaining power of suppliers] and thereby yield a superior return on investment for the firm." It is my contention that strategic thrusts can be used to support or shape the three generic strategies he suggests for outperforming other firms in an industry: *overall cost leadership, differentiation,* and *focus.*

Overall cost leadership requires "aggressive construction of efficient scale facilities, vigorous pursuit of cost reductions from experience, tight cost and overhead control, avoiding marginal customer accounts, and cost minimization in areas like R&D, service, sales force, advertising, and so on. . . . *Low cost relative to competitors* becomes a theme running through the entire strategy."[10] The strategic cost thrust can be used to support or shape this strategy.

But note that Porter's notion of a generic low-cost strategy to defend against the five competitive forces determining industry profitability differs radically from the generic concept of cost as a strategic thrust. For Porter, cost as a generic strategy is not a polar concept; it is defined only with respect to *cost reduction* efforts on the part of a firm following the "overall cost leadership" strategy. The strategic cost thrust suffers no such limitation.

The "second generic strategy is one of differentiating the product or service offering of the firm, creating something that is perceived *industrywide* as being unique. . . . It should be stressed that the differentiation strategy does not allow the firm to ignore costs, but rather they are not the primary *strategic target*."[11] [Italics added.]

Again, note that Porter's notion of a generic differentiation strategy differs radically from the generic concept of differentiation as a strategic thrust. For Porter, differentiation as a generic strategy is not a polar concept; it is defined only with respect to *increasing* the differentiation advantages enjoyed by a firm following this strategy. The strategic differentiation thrust suffers no such limitation.

The final strategy, focus, has as its target a particular industry segment. "The strategy rests on the premise that the firm is thus able to serve its narrow *strategic target* more effectively or efficiently than competitors who are competing more broadly. As a result, the firm achieves either differentiation from better meeting the needs of the particular target, or lower costs in serving this target, or both."[12] The points made above with respect to Porter's other generic strategies apply here as well, since the focus policy relies ultimately on a firm's resolve to be either the low-cost or a highly differentiated producer, albeit in a market segment rather than industrywide.

I have taken pains first to connect and then to distinguish generic strategic thrusts from generic strategies. This done, let us consider another aspect of Porter's work relevant to this book. Recall that generic strategies are designed to cope with the five forces shaping competition and determining (assuming, as Porter does, the truth of the industry structure—behavior—performance model, the fundamental paradigm of industrial organization economics) industry profitability. A firm defends itself against these forces or takes steps to influence them in its favor by adopting a generic strategy that, in Porter's view, will lead to competitive advantage, industrywide or in a particular segment.

The five forces Porter posits derive their strength, which ranges from intense to nil, from a variety of sources. The strategist needs to investigate these sources, for they reveal the strengths and weaknesses of industry participants and environmental opportunities and threats. This study, called structural analysis, provides the base upon which competitive strategy should be formulated. The strategy will attempt to deal with the forces through programs aimed at manipulating their sources. To make this clear and to indicate the role strategic thrusts can play in the process, I shall describe Porter's forces and sources—not in detail but enough for the reader unfamiliar with his work to appreciate its relevance here.

Threat of entry. The strength of this competitive force depends primarily on the height of barriers that must be scaled by a new entrant seeking the potential rewards of industry participation; it also depends upon reactions anticipated from existing competitors. The entry threat is high if barriers are low or severe retaliation is not expected. In general, barriers will be low if an entrant need not invest to match cost savings due to economies of scale, economies of scope (i.e., cost savings attributable to the use of shared resources), economies of experience, and so on. They will also be low if there is no need for the entrant to differentiate the product sold, no cost for customers to switch from an incumbent's product to an entrant's offering, and no difficulty for the entrant in securing access to distribution channels. Finally, barriers will be low if there are no absolute cost disadvantages that the entrant must overcome, such as proprietary technology due to patent protection and favored access of existing competitors to raw materials. In effect, if there are no barriers to entry, existing firms enjoy no competitive advantages. By raising barriers, existing firms acquire either cost or differentiation advantages. Therefore, barriers to entry, if taken as possible strategic moves, reduce to our two strategic thrusts of cost and differentiation. This will become clearer in the next two chapters as these latter concepts are defined and illustrated.

Intensity of rivalry among existing firms. The strength of this competitive force depends on factors often beyond the control of industry participants, such as degree of concentration (in highly concentrated industries, the leader(s) may impose some form of price leadership and therefore avoid intense, no-win competition based solely on price), rate of industry growth (in fast-growth industries, the focal point of strategy is expansion to meet demand, not to outrun other competitors), and lack of switching costs (in industries where product differentiation is low and consequently buyers feel no compunction about changing vendors, severe price competition is the norm). Rivalry is reflected in price competition, advertising battles, new product introduction, and increased customer services. Each of these actions, when part of an organization's competitive strategy, reduces in general to the strategic differentiation thrust.

Pressures from substitute products. The strength of this competitive force depends on the existence of products produced in other industries that customers view as having features similar to those offered by the industry's product(s). In the packaging industry, steel and aluminum manufacturers compete for the business of, for instance, American Can and Continental based on the price and performance features of tin plate and aluminum. In the financial services industry today, the products of brokers, banks, and insurance companies (previously seen as noncompetitive) now vie vigorously for the same investment dollars. Substitute products put limits on industry profitability, as price depends in part on the availability of alternative products offering similar features. To increase this pressure, firms outside the industry must develop product or process innovations. To decrease it, firms in the industry must distinguish their offerings either by price or performance. Such actions reduce to the strategic thrusts of innovation, cost, or differentiation.

Bargaining power of buyers.   "Buyers compete with the industry by forcing down prices, bargaining for higher quality or more services, and playing competitors against each other, all at the expense of industry profitability." The power of this competitive force depends on such factors as whether buyers possess enough information about the supplier's products and operations to prevent it from acting opportunistically with respect to them, pose a credible threat of backward integration, purchase a commodity product (if the product is differentiated, switching costs may reduce the bargaining power of buyers), and so on. Affirmative responses indicate that buyers hold the bargaining power in their negotiations with suppliers. Strategic moves, however, can alter the strength of this force. The strategic thrusts of differentiation, cost, innovation, growth, and alliance can be used to affect the bargaining relation between buyers and suppliers.

Bargaining power of suppliers.   Suppliers compete with buyers over price and product features, each party negotiating or acting to win the best deal, to gain advantage. The strength of this competitive force depends on such factors as whether suppliers possess an information edge that permits them to act opportunistically with respect to buyers, pose a credible threat of forward integration, sell a differentiated product, and so on. Affirmative responses indicate that suppliers possess the bargaining power in their negotiations with buyers. The complete set of strategic thrusts may be used to affect the bargaining relation between suppliers and buyers.

Readers familiar with Porter's work should note that I have omitted discussion of strategic groups, mobility barriers, etc., to avoid unnecessary complexity. These concepts can be easily grasped once the five forces and their sources are understood. Strategic thrusts probably play a greater role vis-à-vis the industry's strategic groups than they do vis-à-vis the industry itself.

This completes the description of the theory of strategic thrusts, the conceptual underpinning for the strategic perspective on information systems. The theory spotlights two complementary lines of strategic thought: Chandler's work on organizational growth and Porter's on competitive analysis. We might visualize these as converging to form a kind of matrix from which the firm fashions its major strategic moves, its strategic thrusts. For, as we have just shown, strategic thrusts are linked directly to Chandler's growth strategies and to Porter's generic strategies and industry forces. They are the basic competitive weapons organizations use in their battles to gain advantage. In the next five chapters I show how information systems are used to support or shape competitive strategy (which includes growth strategies) by supporting or shaping strategic thrusts. Strategic thrusts, therefore, constitute the mechanisms for connecting computers and strategy.

STRATEGIC OPTION GENERATOR

The theory of strategic thrusts enables us not only to illustrate strategic connections but also to design an instrument, the *strategic option generator*, to identify strategic information system opportunities. Strategic thrusts, so to speak, serve as the engine that powers the generator.

The strategic option generator is a conceptual instrument that can be used to identify strategic information systems. But the user must be familiar with the theory of strategic thrusts, just as the experimental physicist who uses a bubble chamber in searching for fundamental particles must grasp the atomic theory of matter. If not, the scientist would, like the layman, see only meaningless patterns instead of particle tracks.

The generator rivets attention first on a range of strategic targets and then on the strategic thrusts that can be used to hit them. Information systems supporting or shaping strategic thrusts, and the thrusts themselves, are *aimed* at strategic targets. By prompting a series of questions related to strategic targets and thrusts, the generator encourages its users to search systematically for strategic information system opportunities.

Three generic classes of strategic target should be explored: suppliers, customers, and competitors. Competitive advantage can be gained with respect to each; in some cases, a strategic thrust and its associated information system can be used to attack multiple targets.

Supplier targets.   The class of supplier targets includes organizations providing what the firm needs to make its product(s) ready for sale, where product is understood to be any good or service offered to satisfy a want or need. This definition is intended to net such diverse production factors as those providing raw materials, finished goods, labor, capital, utilities, insurance, information, advertising and public relations services, energy, permission(s), medical services, transportation, and the like.

Customer targets.   The class of customer targets includes organizations (in the market) that purchase the firm's product for their own use or who sell it, or arrange for its sale, to end users. Again, this definition is intended to capture a wide assortment, including intermediary customers such as:

- Middlemen: Organizations assisting the firm in its search for other customers or in its attempt to close sales with them—e.g., retailers (specialty, department, convenience, combination, discount warehouse, and superstores; supermarkets, service businesses, mail- and telephone-order, vending machines, buying services, door-to-door, chain, franchise operations), wholesalers (full service—wholesale merchants, industrial distributors; limited service—rack jobbers, mail-order, truck jobbers; brokers; agents).
- Physical distributors: Organizations assisting the firm in stocking and moving its products—e.g., truckers, railroads, pipeline companies, airlines, inland and oceanic shippers, bus companies.

- Financial institutions: Organizations assisting the firm in financing its sales or insuring risks associated with their purchase or sale—e.g., banks, credit companies, insurance companies.

End-user customers may be divided into five groups, depending on how they use the firm's product(s):

Consumers: Using it for personal consumption.

Industrial: Using it to produce other products.

Reseller: Using it, after adding value, for resale.

Government: Using it to produce public services, or transferring it to others who need it.

International: Foreign consumers, industrial buyers, resellers, or governments.

Competitor targets. The class of competitor targets includes organizations selling (or potentially selling) products judged, in relation to the firm's, to be the same, similar, or substitutable. Granted, this is not the most precise of definitions. Yet, for our purposes, it is adequate. For it identifies at least three recognizable subclasses: *direct competitors* (also known as "the industry"— those selling the same or similar products, e.g., Ford, GM, Toyota); *potential competitors* (those who may enter the industry to sell the same or similar products); and *substitute competitors* (those selling, or who may sell, substitutable products). To these subclasses, a fourth can be added by extending the definition of competitor targets to include those organizations that may not sell the same, similar, or substitutable products but that may use the same resources (e.g., labor, components) as the firm. I call these *indirect competitors.*

With the diversity of possible supplier, customer, and competitor targets, it is not surprising to find between the firm and these organizations, a variety of transactional relations ranging from long-term contractual to short-term perfunctory, from vehemently competitive to intimately cooperative. Nor is it unusual to discover within the firm specialized groups dedicated to dealing with different kinds of suppliers, customers, and competitors. On the supplier side, for example, we have all observed the human resource function bargaining with labor, telecommunications with long-distance telephone carriers, purchasing with raw materials or finished goods vendors, and so on. On the customer side, we find internal groups dedicated to handling the special needs and desires of intermediary or end-user buyers. In some bargaining negotiations, gaining competitive advantage is the main objective; in others, no such concern dominates.

It is also important to realize that the same kind of agent or intermediary structure may exist between suppliers and the firm as it does between the firm and its customers. Thus, the firm deals in some cases directly with, for instance, manufacturers and in other cases, with sales reps or retailers who may carry the manufacturer's products.

One should note, too, that a firm's suppliers may be its customers or competitors, its competitors may be its suppliers or customers, and its customers may be its suppliers or competitors. This kind of overlap often makes for interesting strategic plays—some legal, others less so.

Finally, the firm's supplier, customer, and competitor relations need to be analyzed to determine opportunities and threats, to decide which are of strategic importance and which can be manipulated by the firm to achieve its ends. I shall return to this subject in the last chapter.

The strategic option generator is used in relation to suppliers, customers, and competitors to generate the largest possible list of strategic targets. It is from this list that the firm selects those that it deems suitable for attack by strategic thrusts supported or shaped by information systems.

From Figure 2–1, it can be seen that the firm has an opportunity to strike in at least 15 generic ways. (This figure should be contrasted with Figure A–2, "Opportunities for Conventional Information Systems, in Appendix A.") With the various subclasses of targets, however, this number rises dramatically. It is further increased by the polarities inherent in strategic thrusts. Two are of particular importance with respect to strategic information systems: mode and direction.

Figure 2-1   Opportunities for strategic information systems

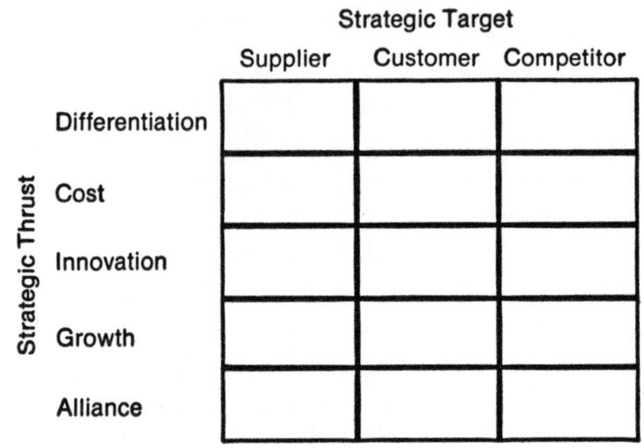

Strategic Target

	Supplier	Customer	Competitor
Differentiation			
Cost			
Innovation			
Growth			
Alliance			

Strategic Thrust

The *mode* of a strategic thrust refers to whether the thrust is used *offensively* to increase an edge or *defensively* to reduce an edge now held by one of the targets. The *direction* of a strategic thrust indicates whether the information system supporting or shaping the thrust is *used* by the firm or *provided* (as such, or in the form of reports generated by the system) to targets.

The option generator (see Figure 2-2) helps expand vastly the search for strategic opportunities to use information systems. When the polarities are counted, the number of generic options rises from 15 (3 × 5) to 60 (3 × 5 × 2 × 2), with the understanding that more opportunities may be generated when various combinations are counted. In my experience, not one firm that has seriously attempted to identify strategic information system opportunities through the use of the option generator has failed to do so. This does not mean, however, that the options discerned (and advantages inherent in them) can be established without commitment of resources. But the generator helps create a substantial number of opportunities systematically. Its purpose is simply to assist users in generating as large a hit list of potential strategic targets as possible.

Figure 2-2   Strategic option generator

What is the strategic target?		
Supplier	Customer	Competitor

What is the strategic thrust?				
Differentiation	Cost	Innovation	Growth	Alliance

What is the mode?	
Offensive	Defensive

What is the direction?	
Use	Provide

It is from this list that the firm selects those it deems suitable for attack by strategic thrusts and information systems.

We have just answered the first question posed by the strategic option generator: What is the strategic target? To address the second—"What is the strategic thrust to be used against the target?"—and the mode and direction questions, we must now consider strategic thrusts in detail, devoting a chapter to each.

BIBLIOGRAPHY

Adams, Walter, ed. *The Structure of American Industry*. 6th ed. New York: Macmillan, 1982.

Chandler, Alfred D., Jr. *Strategy and Structure: Chapters in the History of American Industrial Enterprise*. Cambridge, Mass.: Harvard University Press, 1962.

General Motors. *Annual Reports*. 1925, 1929.

Kotler, Philip. *Marketing Management: Analysis, Planning, and Control*. 5th ed. Englewood Cliffs, N.J.: Prentice-Hall, 1984.

Oxenfeldt, Alfred R., and Jonathan E. Schwartz. *Competitive Analysis*. New York: American Management Association, 1981.

Penrose, Edith T. *The Theory of the Growth of the Firm*. Oxford: Basil Blackwell, 1959.

Porter, Michael E. *Competitive Strategy: Techniques for Analyzing Industries and Competitors*. New York: Free Press, 1980.

Sloan, Alfred P., Jr. *My Years with General Motors*. Garden City, N.Y.: Doubleday Publishing, 1963.

Weiss, Leonard W. *Case Studies in American Industry*. New York: John Wiley & Sons, 1971.

Wiseman, Charles, and Ian MacMillan. "Creating Competitive Weapons from Information Systems." *Journal of Business Strategy*, Fall 1984.

3

Differentiation

PRODUCT DIFFERENTIATION

Potato farmers from Idaho worry about the weather, the cost of new equipment, and the latest government regulation bearing on their crop. Unlike economists, they don't lose sleep computing complex trade-offs between cost and price. If a farmer took his Idaho Grade A's to market and asked for more than the going price, he wouldn't do any business. Buyers don't pay premiums for items they can't distinguish, differentiate, or otherwise discriminate one from the other. Just as the truth value of the sentence "John is a bachelor" remains unchanged when the term *unmarried man* is substituted for *bachelor*, the value for the buyer stays the same when Farmer Jones's peck of Idaho A's is substituted for Farmer Smith's. If you sell a commodity—a standardized, homogenized, substitutable product—you lack the freedom to raise your price above the going rate, assuming you prize solvency. Your customers, moreover, have no reason beside price to prefer your generic product over another's.

For economists, *product differentiation* indicates the degree to which buyers perceive imperfections in the substitutability relation between items offered by sellers in an industry. It is measured by the cross-elasticity of demand. If Product X is highly differentiated from Product Y, a small price reduction in X will not affect demand for Y; if X and Y are close substitutes, a small reduction in the price of X will result in a small increase in the demand for X *and* a small decrease in the demand for Y (assuming the price of Y remains constant), since some customers will switch from Y to X due to the incentive to buy at a reduced price.

Sellers of differentiated goods and services, on the other hand, need to spend time assessing trade-offs between cost, price, and product variation. Differentiation confers on the seller power over these factors, power that can significantly affect profit margin. Yet differentiation has its cost, the price producers must pay when indulging their desire for distinction.

Buyers of differentiated wares also must pay a price when satisfying their preference for something special. Sellers tag differentiated products not only with a price premium but frequently with a loyalty tax, tribute customers may have to pay if they decide to switch from one vendor to another, from Product X to Product Y. The tax will be high if the customer's investment in learning to use X is high, and because it will ipso facto be lost when Y replaces X. In addition, the customer who switches may have to make new investments in learning to use Y. To prevent such infidelities, sellers scheme to raise their customers' *switching costs*; the latter, naturally, take whatever steps they can to minimize such costs.

This situation often creates an opportunity for an enterprising firm to introduce a Product Y designed to reduce the switching costs of prospective customers moving from X to Y *and* to offer desired features or services not associated with X. In the early 60s, Honeywell's Building Controls Group, a supplier of thermostatic and other control systems, seized just this kind of opportunity. Prior to making its strategic move, Honeywell offered to its over 5,000 independent distributors a long line of 18,000 items targeted at both the new and replacement markets. To meet the needs of its intermediaries and their customers, Honeywell maintained a nationwide network of warehouses, for no dealer wanted to stock such a large inventory from a single vendor. Moreover, dealers needed space for competitive lines containing items incompatible with Honeywell's.

To reduce the product differentiation advantages of its competitors as well as its own inventory-carrying and transaction costs, Honeywell executed a bold strategic plan. It redesigned its product line by replacing the 18,000 parts and pieces with 300 interchangeable, standard items. The kicker here was that not only were these interchangeable across Honeywell's product lines but also across those of its major competitors. Through standardization, Honeywell eliminated the differential advantages enjoyed by its rivals.

After this innovation, Honeywell closed its warehouse network and thereby shifted inventory-carrying costs to distributors. The latter assumed the added expense of carrying *all* 300 interchangeable items but would need now to carry fewer items overall. For there was no longer any reason to stock as many competitive substitutes.

Of course, not all distributors went along with Honeywell's strategy. Those that did recorded large sales increases. Honeywell's replacement market share doubled, and its new product sales rose almost 50 percent. Transaction costs declined: Prior to the move, 90 percent of Honeywell's sales had been to 4,000 distributors; within 10 years, that same percentage was sold by 3,100 fewer distributors. This group of 900 also benefited from increased sales volume.

Product differentiation has long been recognized as an important competitive weapon. Indeed, economists who study competitive behavior identify it as one of the principal determinants of advantage. Suppose, for example, that a firm seeks opportunities to diversify into another industry, called A. By analyzing the competitive structure of A, it might find that its potential rivals have neither (1) absolute cost advantages (due to patented-production techniques, unique access to supplies, cheap labor, and so on) nor (2) significant cost advantages (due to economies of scale in production, purchasing, advertising, and the like) nor (3) sustainable product differentiation advantages (due to preferences of buyers for brand name items, superior quality, location, services, and the like). If A is such that participants enjoy neither 1 nor 2 nor 3, the firm can enter A at no disadvantage: competition is pure; no one has an edge.

On the other hand, entry will be blocked or deterred if at least some participants enjoy 1, 2, or 3. To enter this game, a prospective competitor must scale *entry barriers*. And these generally entail costs that put the new entrant, at least initially, at a disadvantage. Product differentiation, in this sense, is a barrier to entry, a long-term deterrent that protects industry incumbents from invasion. It is the study of such barriers and the sources from which their power emanates that occupies a good portion of the industrial economist's time. Among the important sources leading to product differentiation advantages, they have hypothesized such factors as services, physical differences, and subjective image due to brand labeling, advertising, and the like.

Of course, what is one firm's barrier may be another's gateway. When Philip Morris entered the brand-differentiated beer industry through its acquisition of Miller's, it used the advertising hurdle not as a barrier but as a platform, a veritable launching pad for its subsequent conquests. While this obstruction blocked some entrants, it enabled Philip Morris, with its deep financial resources and well-honed marketing skills, to raise Miller's 4 percent market share to well over 20 percent in less than a decade (notwithstanding recent production troubles at Miller's).

The economist's view of product differentiation, reflecting the strong, narrow sense of the term, differs from the somewhat weaker, wider meaning ascribed to it by marketers. The latter have operationalized the economist's theoretical insights by deriving a variety of schemes, all going under the name "marketing mix," aimed at systematically uncovering opportunities to make their products unique and thereby establish differential advantage over their rivals.

When first proposed by Borden in 1964, the term *marketing mix* covered not only possible combinations of such marketing elements as product quality, price, and channel of distribution but also the market forces determining management's choice of a combination to satisfy the firm's profit and growth objectives. For Borden, the *elements* comprised policies and procedures related to: product planning (product lines offered, markets to sell, new products), pricing, branding, distribution channels, personal selling, advertising, promotion, packaging, display, servicing, physical distribution, and fact-finding and analysis (securing, analyzing, and using the facts needed to make marketing decisions). The *forces* determining a mix of the elements included consumers' buying behavior and its determinants, the trade's (wholesalers', retailers') behavior and its influences, competitors' position and behavior and its influences (e.g., industry structure, relation of supply to demand, degree to which competitors compete on a price versus nonprice basis, technological trends), and government behavior and its market impact.

Since Borden's work, others have attempted to refine the notion, restricting its sense to the marketing-mix elements. Albert Frey, for example, proposes two categories: the offering (product, packaging, brand, price, and service) and methods and tools (distribution channels, personal selling, advertising, sales, promotion, and publicity). William Lazer and Eugene Kelley suggest three: goods-and-services mix, distribution mix, and communications mix. Jerome McCarthy touts four: product (quality, features, options, style, brand name, packaging, sizes, services, warranties, returns), price (list, discounts, allowances, payment period, credit terms), place (channels, coverage, locations, inventory, transport), and promotion (advertising, personal selling, sales promotion, publicity).

By adopting one of these marketing-mix schemata, the firm positions itself to manipulate a large number of variables. This yields an even larger number of possible marketing combinations, each capable of establishing a differential edge. Take the case of a single product. If its quality can be excellent, good, or fair; if its price ranges from $50 to $150 in increments of $10; if it is distributed through retail, wholesale, or company-owned outlets; and if its promotion takes the form of either local demonstrations or advertisements via newspaper, magazine, radio, television, or mail; then there are 594 (3 × 11 × 3 × 6) possible marketing mixes, that is, ways to establish differential advantage.

This brief review of the concept of product differentiation, from first the economist's and then the marketer's perspective, is sufficient for my purpose here, which is to elucidate the strategic thrust of differentiation and show how information systems can be used to support or shape it. The cases described below fall into three classes: differentiation of expected product, differentiation of augmented product, and marketing support for differentiated products.

DIFFERENTIATION: EXPECTED PRODUCT

Information systems used to support or shape the firm's expected product do so with respect to such marketing-mix elements as:

- Delivery (Are customers' expectations met with respect to quantity of product, time of delivery, channel of distribution?).

- Terms (Is credit extended? Are allowances made?).
- Support (Is advice available before, during, and after sale?).

The firm's *expected product*, the offering it designs to satisfy the customer's minimal buying conditions (as just indicated), includes all those characteristics intrinsic to the *generic product*, the basic, plain vanilla offering that competitors may find no difficulty in emulating. Even at the generic level, opportunities to differentiate exist. But they are much more plentiful once one moves beyond the unadorned to the anticipated (i.e., expected), as suppliers of perfumes and other cosmetic products seem to understand intuitively. According to Levitt, "the generic product can be sold only if the customer's wider expectations are met. Different means may be employed to meet these expectations. Hence differentiation follows expectation."

When industrial buyers, and perhaps others as well, assess a vendor's offering, they weigh heavily such virtues as reliable delivery, prompt quotation, technical advice, discounts, maintenance, sales representation, credit, and ease of contact. Each should be carefully explored as potential strategic information systems (SIS) opportunity areas.

In the 70s, Warren Communication, a manufacturer of power supplies for telephone systems, and Corning Glass, a multiproduct manufacturer of glass-related products, learned the same lesson: Prompt delivery is an aspect of service in which a firm can use information systems to shape a differentiation thrust and gain an edge. Both companies discovered this truth only after suffering the pangs of competitive disadvantage. Warren—with a 12 percent share in an industry led by AT&T's Western Electric—supplied telecommunications companies, governments, and others. Its former president recalls that because of late and generally mediocre delivery performance, Warren paid $140,000 in 1980 in late-charge penalties, infuriated customers like GTE and MCI, and lost $3 million in contracts canceled by the governments of Taiwan and Puerto Rico for failure to deliver.

At Corning's Erwin ceramics plant the story was slightly different, but the pressure to produce on time was just as, if not more, intense. Erwin, a major source of catalytic converter components, supplied parts to manufacturers such as Ford and Chrysler for use in their automobile emission control systems. In 1979, a Japanese-based division of NCK–Locke Inc., with a 20 percent share of the market, introduced an improved version of its product and gained an additional 10 percent share. Erwin, the market leader, had to act to protect its position.

At Warren and Erwin, the response was the same. Both installed information systems to improve the management of their manufacturing operations, from loading to shipping dock. At Warren, the system eliminated late-delivery penalties, restored customer confidence, and led to a doubling of plant capacity. At Corning, enhanced quality control *plus* improved performance in delivery (the delivery success rate for the first three quarters of 1983 was measured at 99.8 percent) enabled the firm to repulse the Japanese attack. According to NGK's Ceramic Division manager, "We cannot offer the same lead time as Corning. Our product is produced overseas, and it is shipped by boat. The shipping, customs, and trucking slow delivery."

Savvy customers often apply another test to the offerings of suppliers: Can they provide prompt, clear, and accurate quotations? This condition tends frequently to separate winners from also-rans. Taking the hint, firms large and small have developed information systems applications to satisfy precisely this service need of their clients.

The president of Rehler, Vaughn, Beaty & Koone, an architectural firm based in San Antonio, Texas, knew that "to get ahead of the competition, we would have to learn to use a microcomputer." His firm developed cost-estimating and income property analysis applications so that it could generate for prospective clients estimates for different structures occupying the same space. After collecting client responses to questions about quality of materials, location, building type, and so forth, Rehler's program produced detailed reports on costs, schedules, projected income and expenses, return on investment, and the like. Because of its ability to provide quick, reliable quotes, Rehler recovered from customers attracted to its service more than 10 times what it had invested in systems.

For Setco Industries, a supplier of machine-tool components, the speed of its computer-aided engineering system means the difference between winning contracts or losing them. Due to Setco's ability to generate quotations in hours rather than days, sales have doubled. Its president notes that on one job, "we had the order before our competitor ever had a chance to quote it."

Continuing now in a more theatrical vein, Olesen of Hollywood, a rental supplier of lighting equipment to film production companies, uses its minicomputer system not only to handle inventory but also to build customer credibility and avoid confrontations. Prior to implementing the application, according to Olesen's president, "the same information scribbled on a piece of paper would most likely initiate an argument. The system convinces the customer that we are a first-class operation and that they are dealing with professionals. This makes them happy and comfortable." Olesen's information system gives it a differential edge in the fiercely competitive theatrical rental equipment business.

Friedman & Associates, a custom software vendor based in Deerfield, Illinois, develops order entry, manufacturing control, purchasing, and related on-line applications. It differentiates these offerings from the hundreds of similar if not identical products on the market by providing a special feature. Instead of having users carry, store, and search through thick manuals of documentation, Friedman in 1982 became one of the first firms to offer an on-line documentation feature with its packages. For any of the applications just mentioned, puzzled users need only press a HELP key on the terminal and easy-to-read text is flashed on the screen to aid them.

A somewhat more controversial use of information systems to differentiate a firm's expected product comes from the securities industry. Portfolio managers hired by corporations, unions, and state and local governments to invest money for pension funds can accumulate "soft dollars" from brokers who charge more than the lowest possible rate for a securities transaction. This practice is justified because the law doesn't require money managers to trade with the broker offering the cheapest commission, as long as investment research is included.

Inventive brokers have interpreted the term *investment research* broadly to include one-week, all-expenses-paid trips to Paris, Madrid, and Milan; tickets to sports and cultural events; meetings with influential political and government figures, and so on. Others have seen an opportunity to enhance their expected research offering by providing computer terminals with sophisticated analytical investment programs. For some clients, it seems, such rewards are more appealing than a week on the French Riviera.

Up to this point, I have presented only examples of the offensive use of information systems to support or shape strategic differentiation thrusts. The air traffic controller's strike of 1981 illustrates the defensive use of information systems to reduce the differentiation advantages of labor—in this case, the controllers.

The federal government based its decision to dismiss the strikers in part on the availability of a computer application for controlling the flow of aircraft. According to labor relations expert Harley Shaiken of MIT, what doomed the strike was the "government's skillful use of a new weapon—information systems technology—to keep air traffic moving, gutting the strikers' leverage." Soon after the walkout, 75 percent of the commercial flights were operating while 75 percent of the controllers were marching on the picket line.

Prior to striking, controllers were considered to be highly trained specialists, in short supply. By performing many of the controller's tasks, the flow-control system dramatically reduced their bargaining power, making the skills they had less valuable. (As labor's skill differentiation advantages erode, its price on the market drops.) The system also widened the pool of new applicants by reducing the level of expertise required.

DIFFERENTIATION: AUGMENTED PRODUCT

Information systems used to support or shape the firm's *augmented* product do so with respect to marketing-mix elements that reach beyond the customer's minimal expectations. Whatever benefits the customer and can be added to the expected product should be examined by the firm as an opportunity for a differentiation thrust. From this set of options, those that can be supported or shaped by information systems should be identified and assessed.

Pacific Intermountain Express (PIE), a large trucking firm based in California, competes in the deregulated, commoditylike trucking industry. It developed an application for tracking the status of a shipment at any point along its route from origin to destination. A PIE customer checks on its misplaced or delayed shipment by querying the PIE computer, using its own computer terminal.

Through this information system, PIE differentiates its shipping service from the noncomputerized ones offered by its rivals. As the company's president put it, "In trucking today, we all use the same highways and the same freight terminals. Our only competitive advantage is to stand out technologically."

Back in 1971, PIE seized the opportunity to set itself apart from the 15,000 competing firms in the industry by investing in an on-line computer system for shipment tracing and freight billing. Today, PIE offers to its customers reports on over-the-road costs and empty-mile cost allocation. It allows them to send and receive a variety of messages related to their shipments. When PIE's vice president for marketing visits clients, he discusses not only shipping volumes and rates but also information system requirements. These meetings inspire many of the system's enhancements. At the request of a GM plant manager in California, for instance, PIE developed an application that lists all inbound shipments due on its trucks. Like Metpath in the clinical laboratory business, PIE raised the information systems ante for other trucking firms through the strategic use of computer technology.

In the past, furnituremakers competed against one another on the basis of style, color, price, and other features. Today, a new source of competitive advantage is emerging in the service area. With computer-aided design (CAD) systems, interior designers can simulate alternative furniture arrangements from a variety of perspectives. Manufacturers view CAD systems as important new marketing tools. "We're doing this to support our business," says a vice president and director of marketing for Steelcase Inc., a large,

Michigan-based furniture company. Steelcase developed software to display its product line and sell to its dealers. A competitor, Herman Miller, decided to go toe to toe with Steelcase, implementing a $250,000 top-of-the-line system. With it, designers can pan across a roomful of furniture. According to Herman Miller's program manager, to compare other systems to it "is like comparing snapshots to a movie."

Epson, a manufacturer of dot-matrix printers, personal computers, and handheld computers, offers a set of computer-based services to its distributors, retailers, and end users. To strengthen its bonds with these groups, Epson contracted with CompuServe, Inc. for space on its new videotex network. Callers connect their computers with CompuServe through a local dial-up number. Only Epson's intermediaries can download technical and pricing information about product lines, read Epson's electronic newsletter, and correspond via electronic mail. Others can access public files for news and feature stories about Epson's products or participate in conference calls to exchange information. These services help Epson differentiate its product line by augmenting it through the use of information systems provided by CompuServe.

Hertz, the car rental agency, and Owens-Corning Fiberglass, the home-insulation company, also use systems to augment their expected products. Each offers its customers reports pertaining precisely to their needs. The Hertz customized printout explains in English, French, German, Italian, or Spanish (depending on the language preference of the traveler) how to reach hotels, office buildings, convention sites, and sports arenas in major U.S. cities. Once the traveler specifies the destination desired, it details expressways and exits, where to turn, and how long the trip should take.

To differentiate its commodity-like product line, Owens-Corning hit upon a distinctive computer-based service. Home buyers, it knew, wanted well-insulated houses. But they lacked convenient, inexpensive tests for assessing the energy efficiency of designs proposed by builders. This presented a challenging opportunity for Owens-Corning: What can we do to satisfy the obvious consumer want and get our buyers, the builders, to select our products rather than those of our competitors?

By design or chance, it responded to this challenge ingeniously with an information system for cranking out energy efficiency ratings for new home designs. Owens-Corning offers the package "free" to builders as a service for their customers, the home buyers. In return, Owens-Corning makes two demands on builders: carry only our insulation materials and meet minimum efficiency standards in design. While the jury still sits on this attempt to build customer loyalty and increase sales, I believe it represents a strategic thrust that warrants emulation in other industries as well.

Along these lines, Benjamin Moore, the paint company, developed a computerized paint analyzer for retail stores selling its products. Janovic/Plaza, an independent paints and papers, blinds, and fabrics store in New York City, recently ran an advertisement headlined "Get 50 percent off Levolor Blinds and a Computer to Match." What Janovic meant here was that a customer could select any of Levolor's 100-plus colors and then use its (i.e., Moore's) computer color matching system to determine the exact paint-mix formula needed for matching the blinds with Moore's paint. Janovic also offered this augmented service for matching fabric swatches, wallpaper, or whatever.

Consider now a use of information systems to reduce the differentiation advantages of competitors. In the cosmetics industry, firms like Chanel, Clinique, and Revlon spend millions each year on advertizing to establish brand name identity, to differentiate themselves from the swarms of other companies in the business. Without a large advertizing budget, a new firm (so the conventional wisdom goes) would find it difficult to enter this highly competitive marketplace.

In 1984, three cosmetics companies introduced computer systems to analyze human skin, simulate how different makeup will look, and instruct on applying their products. Two firms, Shiseido and Intelligent Skincare (hardly household words) unveiled their systems at Bloomingdale's, the large New York City department store. According to the store's executive vice president, customer response was remarkable. "Yesterday, 70 people were standing around looking at the demonstrations. Shiseido has quintupled its sales. And to our astonishment, I.S.—a totally unknown company—has been very strong." It seems that these two companies have learned the trick of effective retailing: getting customers to their counter, not to their rival's.

AT&T's flaunting of its Unix operating system suggests another example of a defensive differentiation thrust involving an augmented product. Somewhat analogous to Honeywell's strategic move in the control market (described earlier), this also has an offensive kicker.

Unix emerged from the research of two computer scientists in one of the back rooms at Bell Labs during the late 60s. It has two remarkable strategic features: horizontal and vertical portability. This means that Unix runs on the machines of competing computer manufacturers (horizontal portability) and on micros, minis, and mainframes (vertical portability). Defined on over 70 different types of computers, it can be used to operate IBM, Sperry, Amdahl, and Honeywell mainframes; Digital Equipment, Data General, and Hewlett-Packard minicomputers; and microcomputers driven by Intel, Zilog, and Motorola chips. AT&T's recently announced lines of mainframe and minicomputers, not surprisingly, run under Unix.

Why is AT&T touting the virtues of Unix? Listen to the explanation proffered by the vice president of computer systems at AT&T Technologies, Inc.:

> We're anxious to see IBM and other companies go with our *standard*. We think it's good for the whole industry. A lot of the industry infrastructure—the value-added resellers—agrees with that. It's been our product for a long time, and I think the industry has been pretty successful going with our *standard*. If IBM goes another way, that will be unfortunate because it will have a diversifying effect on the industry. [Italics added.][13]

AT&T's beneficence rings even more resonantly in the words of the head of Unix Systems Planning at Bell Labs:

> The Bell system telephone network is made up of many different machines running many different operating systems. It is a distributed operating system that we have managed to develop and continue to

evolve. The Unix system is like that. It provides a uniform tying factor from micros to mainframes which the industry can capitalize on to get to the consumer market.

And consumers can capitalize, too, because now they have access to microcomputers. There are different machines, different operating systems, different interfaces—they're very confusing to customers. The automobile industry solved that problem quite well—that's a very complex device that many of us can run. There are not that many people who can run computers. I think we need to provide a basis for solving that problem, and I think the Unix system provides that basis very well.[14]

But is this the whole story behind AT&T's extraordinary advertising and public relations campaign on behalf of its Unix baby, Ma Bell's first legitimate offspring since divestiture? Not by a long shot. The computer industry recognizes no operating-system standards except local, de facto ones, primarily established by IBM. Why? Because operating systems are one of the best investments a computer vendor can make in locking in its customer base, in raising customer switching costs to a painfully high level. Imagine what it would be like if a firm could move all its applications from, for instance, IBM to AT&T computers, with no switching cost except small change? As the poet Ezra Pound once mused: "America, America. Think what America would be like if the classics had a wide circulation." IBM, I'm sure, has thought about what the world would be like if AT&T's Unix had a wide circulation. I leave it as an exercise for the reader to predict the final outcome of this bold strategic thrust by the former monopolistic giant, reincarnated now as the information industry's David.

DIFFERENTIATION: MARKETING SUPPORT

Finally, information systems used to support or shape other marketing efforts do so with respect to activities related to the firm's differentiated product(s). As the following cases show, these activities include but are not limited to product line planning, market planning, media selection, product promotion, R&D, and production.

According to E. F. Hutton, packaged investments accounted for 30 percent of its commission revenues in 1983, up from 4 percent in 1978. Unlike traditional stocks or bonds, these bundled, often unique products target competitive offerings. Financial service firms like Hutton use information systems as integral parts of their product creation or "manufacturing" processes.

Consider, for example, how one large firm created a new certificates of deposit (CD) fund. At 6 A.M., traders at the brokerage house called London to order sheafs of CDs from foreign banks, which often pay higher rates than their U.S. counterparts. By 11 A.M., they had accumulated $50 million of the paper. The next step in the fund creation process depended on an information system that took the prices and rates, juggled them according to the firm's objectives and constraints embodied in its computer program, and arrived at management fees and commissions. Thirty-six hours after the start of this production run (job-shop style, to be sure), brokers were selling the fund.

Behind all the promotional hoopla surrounding such products, there is generally an information system playing a critical role in product development, processing, or distribution. A computerized portfolio management system, for example, directs Shearson/ American Express's managed-commodity account. Merrill's Cash Management Account (see below) depends for its existence on database and laser printing technology.

Scholastic Magazine, unlike the financial services firms just mentioned, uses its information system to support product- and market-planning efforts. Due to decreasing school enrollments and budgets, the 60-year-old publisher of elementary and secondary school materials faces mounting pressures to develop and market new products in the 80s.

To meet the challenges, the company compiled an automated data base with information on its product sales, on 16,000 school districts, on teachers and students who have bought its products, on millions of U.S. households (obtained from data on census tracts), and so on. This marketing information system produces sales penetration ratios (e.g., sales/teacher, sales/student etc.), district profiles, and the like.

Scholastic uses the system to fine-tune the personal selling efforts of its approximately 100 sales representatives. But its most critical application relates to direct mail campaigns, the firm's major method of reaching the school market. *Scholastic* posts over 50 million items a year, using its marketing information system as one would a rifle's telescopic lens. Without it, like competitors who lack such a system, *Scholastic* would be shooting in the dark. But with it, *Scholastic* can, with a high degree of confidence, support efforts to develop differentiated products and the plans to market them to well-defined segments and customer groups.

Along similar lines, the United Church of Christ (UCC), faced with declining membership, has put its faith in the power of information systems to attract new or past members to its flock. Using data from 1980 census tracts on such variables as age, income level, ethnic background, and so on, the UCC can, with a few simple computer programs, create a demographic profile of a community. With this profile as a guide, the UCC pastor can devise targeted programs to capture recent immigrants, the elderly, yuppies, or what have you. But the UCC doesn't have an exclusive here. Religious battles for market share are brewing as other church groups mobilize their forces. The United Presbyterian Church, for example, has its own programmers and access to computers at Concordia College in River Forest, Illinois. According to the director of research for the church, "We can build an age-sex pyramid [an interesting idea as such], determine how many people are bilingual, and determine the educational level in any census tract."

While demographic analysis suits the needs of *Scholastic* and UCC to identify prospects, Manufacturers Hanover Trust (MHT), the nation's fourth largest bank-holding company (based in New York) takes a different track. In 1977, it sponsored the first corporate challenge race (3.5 miles) in Central Park, attracting 600 entrants. Within six years, it ran (at the New York City Park Department's behest) three heats of no more than 10,000 runners each and started races in Los Angeles, San Francisco, Houston, Dallas, Atlanta, Albany, Buffalo, Syracuse, and Chicago.

What happened at a recent run in Houston is typical of the entire MHT program. The race turned up 12 companies considered to be active prospects. After-race contact could be easily established, as MHT people knew members of the target's running team personally. This isn't a random kind of thing—it's designed into the program. According to a senior vice president and director of marketing for the bank, the name, company, and corporate position of all runners in a race become part of a data base from which MHT and its subsidiaries in factoring, international banking, leasing, and the like, draw leads. At $30,000 a shot, the vice president claims that these races provide "the biggest bang for the buck in our whole marketing effort." It must be particularly gratifying for MHT to see runners from its competitors—Citibank, Chase, and Chemical—pin "Manufacturer Hanover Corporate Challenge" identification tags to their running outfits and give their all for good old Manny Hanny.

To support the promotional component of the marketing mix—advertising, personal selling, sales promotion, and publicity—firms use information systems in a variety of inventive applications. In the increasingly international and competitive game of commercial real estate, developers new to an area help prospective tenants visualize structures still on the drawing board by inviting them to elaborate shows held at "marketing centers." To induce tenants reluctant to lease space unseen, builders create Hollywood-style productions to simulate planned structures. Gerald Hines Interests, a Houston-based developer seeking a foothold in the Manhattan market, was the first to use this new marketing tool to sell space in large commercial complexes. Recently, to attract New York City tenants to its site on 53rd Street, Hines presented a show driven by 24 computer-controlled slide projectors. According to some in this field, "If we lease the project three weeks sooner because of the marketing center, we've paid for it." In southern and western markets, builders view marketing centers as essential. Indeed, they would not initiate a project without them. And information systems have become indispensable to these elaborate promotional efforts.

For companies that must undergo the rigors of competitive bidding, the bid itself can be viewed as a product, intermediate to be sure, but just as important (if not more so) than the final product. For if the bid is not bought, everything else must remain on the shelf. This applies to products the firm offers for sale as well as to those items it seeks to acquire through the bidding process. Firms engaged in competitive bidding battles must be adept at the intricate details of negotiating, entertaining, politicking, maneuvering, and analyzing. Some, like Sun Oil and Otis Elevator, have learned to use information systems in supporting their winning bids.

Sun competes against other oil exploration firms for offshore leases. This is not a game for the timid or the ignorant, involving as it does huge amounts of money and high levels of risk. When the U.S. government recently sold $1 billion worth of offshore tracts in the Gulf of Mexico, Sun successfully bid on 35 of the 48 blocks it wanted, paying $22 million. To "take the risk out of the crapshoot," says the manager of planning and analysis, Sun developed an information system application to help price its bids, taking into consideration such variables as reserve estimates, oil price forecasts, and drilling and development costs. The system acts as a filter; in the recent bidding, it eliminated as too costly 15 of the 66 tracts that had satisfied geological criteria as possible sites for exploration.

Otis, on the other hand, developed an information system to provide strategic intelligence on the competition. The system tracks all elevator sales put out for bid, about 50 a day, in the United States. The national sales director for Otis says that "when we know that a job exists, it is posted on the system, and we start negotiating. When it is in the budget stage, we give it a dollar value and then keep track of it through the bid and contract dates." Having this information available, Otis is able to compare systematically its prices with those of the competition and thereby to improve significantly its chances for developing winning bids.

CASE REFERENCES

Air Traffic Controllers　*Computerworld*, April 5, 1982.

AT&T　*Computerworld*, August 22, 1983; December 26, 1983; January 2, 1984; January 23, 1984; January 30, 1984; March 12, 1984; *Information Systems News*, February 7, 1983; December 12, 1983; January 23, 1984; February 6, 1984.

Benjamin Moore Paint　*New York Times*, 1984, advertisement.

Brokers　*The Wall Street Journal*, October 4, 1984.

CompuServe　See Epson.

Corning Glass　*Manufacturing Technology: A Report to Management.*

Epson　*Communications Week*, July 16, 1984.

Friedman & Associates　*Computerworld*, August 16, 1982.

Gerald Hines　*The Wall Street Journal*, August 7, 1984.

Herman Miller　*Business Week*, July 5, 1982.

Hertz　*The Wall Street Journal*, April 24, 1984.

Honeywell　Levitt, *Marketing for Business Growth* (see Bibliography to this chapter).

E. F. Hutton　*The Wall Street Journal*, March 29, 1983.

Intelligent SkinCare　*New York Times*, October 21, 1984; October 29, 1984.

Manufacturers Hanover　*Business Week*, August 22, 1983.

Miller's　*New York Times*, August 27, 1984; Yip, *Barriers to Entry: A Corporate Strategic Perspective* (see Bibliography to this chapter).

Olesen　*The Office*, September 1981.

Otis Elevator   *Output,* May 1981.

Owens-Corning Fiberglass   *Business Week,* August 22, 1983.

Pacific Intermountain Express   *Distribution,* September 1981; *Management Information System Week,* March 24, 1982.

Rehler, Vaughn, Beaty & Koone   *Output,* June 1981.

Scholastic Magazine   *Computerworld,* November 30, 1981.

Setco Industries   *American Machinist,* June 1982.

Shearson/American Express   *The Wall Street Journal,* March 29, 1983.

Shiseido   See Intelligent SkinCare.

Steelcase   See Herman Miller.

Sun Oil   *The Wall Street Journal,* July 19, 1984.

United Church of Christ   *New York Times,* October 23, 1982.

Warren Communications   See Corning Glass.

BIBLIOGRAPHY

Bain, Joe S. *Barriers to New Competition.* Cambridge, Mass.: Harvard University Press, 1956.

_____. *Industrial Organization.* 2d ed. New York: John Wiley & Sons, 1968.

Borden, Neil H. "The Concept of the Marketing Mix." *Journal of Advertising Research,* June 1964.

Caves, Richard. *American Industry: Structure, Conduct, Peformance.* 4th ed. Englewood Cliffs, N.J.: Prentice-Hall, 1977.

Frey, Albert W. *Advertising.* 3d ed. New York: Ronald Press, 1961.

Kotler, Philip. *Marketing Management: Analysis, Planning, and Control.* 5th ed. Englewood Cliffs, N.J.: Prentice-Hall, 1984.

Lazer, William, and Eugene J. Kelley. *Managerial Marketing: Perspectives and Viewpoints.* Rev. ed. Homewood, Ill.: Richard D. Irwin, 1962.

Levitt, Theodore. *Marketing for Business Growth.* New York: McGraw-Hill, 1974.

_____. "Marketing Success through Differentiation—of Anything." *Harvard Business Review,* January–February, 1980.

McCarthy, Jerome E. *Basic Marketing: A Managerial Approach.* 7th ed. Homewood, Ill.: Richard D. Irwin, 1981.

Porter, Michael E. *Competitive Strategy.* New York: Free Press, 1980.

Yip, George S. *Barriers to Entry: A Corporate Strategy Perspective.* Lexington, Mass.: D. C. Heath, 1982.

4

Cost

COST ECONOMIES

Just as competitive advantage may flow to the firm concentrating its strategic moves on product differentiation, it may also issue to the organization focusing its thrusts on cost economies. For the imaginative enterprise, the latter presents a fertile field of opportunity. Rather than attempt to map it completely (which would require us to cover such economic exotica as X-efficiency theory, a theory that attempts to account for the difference "between the value of maximizing the opportunities open to the firm and those actually utilized" by it), I shall limit the discussion to three important kinds of cost savings: economies of scale, scope, and information. It's with reference to these that enterprising firms can fashion a variety of strategic thrusts, thrusts that frequently can be supported or shaped by information systems.

Strategic cost thrusts are strategic moves intended to reduce or avoid costs the firm would otherwise incur, to help suppliers or customers reduce or avoid costs so that the firm receives preferential treatment or other benefits it deems worthwhile, or to increase the costs of its competitors.

Following the pattern established in the preceding chapter, I shall review the basics of scale, scope, and information economies and then show through examples how strategic information systems can be used in conjunction with each.

COST: SCALE

Scale economies enable relatively large firms to acquire, produce, process, store, ship, or sell products at lower cost per unit than relatively small ones. Opportunities to reap the rewards of economies based on size may be seen from the perspective of the firm's functional activities (e.g., manufacturing, marketing, and purchasing) or may be viewed from the vantage point of its products, plants, or multiplant operations. In most industries, up to a certain point, economies of scale may be attained if the firm is willing and able to make the necessary investments. Once minimum optimal scale—the smallest size at which average cost per unit is at its lowest—is reached, however, any move to increase the size of a firm's operation would most likely result in diseconomies of scale, higher costs caused by such factors as rising transport charges, lack of local labor, and bureaucratic inefficiencies.

What accounts for the possibility of scale economies? What kinds of action are open to a large firm but closed to a small one? What are the sources of increased efficiency, of lowered average unit cost? Among the factors most frequently cited by economists are the following:

Specialization.   As Adam Smith observed over 200 years ago, efficiency can be increased if labor is divided. Ideally, the firm meshes requirements of the job, abilities of the worker, and wages paid, so that employees are kept busy all the time at tasks demanding all their faculties. By taking advantage of Smith's division of labor principle, large firms avoid the waste and cost of having skilled, highly paid employees performing tasks which less-qualified, lower-paid workers could do as well if not better. Size enables them to employ specialized labor for well-defined jobs.

Automation.   With ever-finer divisions of labor and concommitant specialization, opportunities increase to automate particular tasks or entire processes. Large firms can take advantage of these opportunities more readily than their smaller counterparts, as they have the resources to invest in specialized equipment designed to increase efficiency.

Bargaining power.   Large firms, because of the size of their orders, shipments, or service needs, frequently are able to cut better deals with suppliers, customer intermediaries, and end users than those negotiated by their smaller rivals. Volume discounts on purchases, transportation, and so on, are well-known instances of this source of scale economy.

Failures of proportionality.   A large firm can frequently capitalize on certain failures of proportionality. Capacity increases can often be achieved at less than proportionate rises in equipment or labor costs. As the number of machines at a facility increases, the number of technicians needed for maintenance usually rises less than proportionately.

Experience.   Large firms are able to take advantage of unit cost declines due to cumulative volume increases—the so-called experience curve effect. Such declines are the result of learning, of the experience workers gain in mastering their jobs, the machines they use, and so on. Their learning generally results in increases in the rate of output and in decreases in the rate of errors.

But we must remember that these and other sources of scale economies may also turn into sources of diseconomies. The large firm with a highly specialized labor force cannot easily retrain it if forced by a drastic decline in demand to exit from its primary business and enter a new arena. The long-term price contract that was the envy of the industry when consummated between the largest manufacturer and its principal raw material supplier may not be worth the paper it's printed on, indeed may cost the manufacturer far in excess of the price of the contract, if technological innovation makes a cheaper, easily substitutable material available. Similarly, the newly built 20-acre, rural processing plant that takes optimum advantage of a proportionality failure may find it lacks the labor willing to work in such an environment. Or, the firm that has invested heavily in technology designed to improve the productivity of its labor force and hence its opportunity to ride the experience curve, may find other firms using new and less costly techniques to produce in far greater volume, with order-of-magnitude increases in quality. Like most strategic thrusts, moves to exploit economies of scale cut both ways. Caveat emptor.

While the idea of scale economies may bring forth images of gigantic blast ovens and massive rolling mills, it would be a mistake to believe that such savings were restricted to heavy industry. Through the strategic use of information systems, banks, hospitals, and other organizations have capitalized on scale economies inherent in their lines of business.

In 1982, Chase Manhattan Corporation acquired the Visa traveler's check business of the First National Bank of Chicago. In this activity, profit comes mainly from the float, the funds which issuing institutions like American Express, Citicorp, Barclay's, and Chase invest between the time a traveler's check is purchased and redeemed. According to banking sources, industry leader American Express has at its disposal on an average day $2 billion in float; invested at 15 percent, this would yield a gross of over $300 million a year.

But since check-processing overhead is high, large volume is necessary to clear a significant profit. This reason evidently motivated Chase's purchase decision, for the acquisition doubled its annual traveler's check sales volume to over $1 billion and its sales outlets (primarily other banks) to about 10,000. According to a Chase vice president, it "gives us *economies of scale* faster than we could get through internal growth. It will reduce our cost per check by 20 percent." Like the expensive steel press whose cost is spread over as many units as possible, the cost of Chase's large-scale information systems operation can now be spread over a volume sufficient enough to reduce its average cost per transaction by one fifth.

Taking advantage of proportionality failures in data processing operations and a fortuitous chain of events, General Bancshares Corp., until recently a relatively small, St. Louis–based bank involved primarily in selling home mortgages and local loans, has also benefited from scale economies. When federal law prohibited interstate banking in 1956, a loophole permitted banks with interstate holdings at the time to keep them. General Bancshares opted to retain its units in Illinois and Tennessee. In 1982, these two states passed laws permitting bank-holding companies within the state to expand. General Bancshares acquired Belleville National Bank of Illinois and reduced local marketing and auditing expenses, using corporate resources. In addition, it eliminated the redundant data processing operation at Belleville and thereby cut over $750,000 from Belleville's annual overhead because of the services its centralized, large-scale information systems group could offer.

American Medical International, a large hospital management firm, saw a similar opportunity to exploit a failure of proportionality when it acquired Lifemark, another concern in its industry. According to the president of Lifemark, "the key to understanding this transaction is the rather dramatic *economies of scale* that will result. Over $20 million of Lifemark headquarters expense will be eliminated annually. There'll be a $10 million saving in data-processing costs." Indeed, rising costs in the health care industry have, according to some, made size an essential ingredient for survival.

Humana, the second largest hospital chain in the United States, certainly appreciates the opportunities for scale economies supported by information systems. A senior vice president notes that "a key element in our growth is the computer." He expects the information systems staff to increase from its 1983 level of 350, a sevenfold jump from 1973, to at least 700 in another 10 years. This group enables Humana to develop large, centralized information systems and to spread costs over the more than 89 hospitals Humana runs. A recently installed system to manage inventory is expected to save Humana over $85 million in labor and reduced expenditures in three years.

Regional securities firms face rising competition from commercial banks and national brokerage houses. A significant revenue source, the underwriting of municipal revenue bonds, is threatened by the entry of banks into their business with the advent of deregulation. Customer bases face erosion as growing numbers are lured by costly, technological-based products offered by such firms as Merrill Lynch. When Merrill was attracting 10,000 customers a week with its Cash Management Account, the president of a regional acknowledged that his firm didn't have the resources to offer a similar product.

Situations like this represent opportunities for growth-minded companies like Shearson/American Express, the brokerage subsidiary of American Express. In 1982, Shearson acquired Foster & Marshall of Seattle, the Northwest's leading regional. According to Mr. Foster, the head of the company, plans for expansion and the need to enhance its data processing system were among his most important merger motives. From Shearson's point of view, the acquisition expanded the market for its products (by adding Foster's customer base) and enabled it to achieve economies of scale by integrating Foster's data processing operations into its own.

Levitz, the large furniture retailer, capitalized on information systems to support a strategic cost thrust that dramatically improved its bargaining position with its suppliers. Rather than have its local outlets (cash-and-carry warehouses stocking items on display) deal directly with vendors, Levitz established a 12-person buying department at corporate headquarters in Miami. Supported by a system that allows local store managers to identify slow-moving items, cut prices, and increase turn ratios, the central staff can restock simply by checking items off a master list. The president at Levitz, in commenting on the strategic significance of the system, remarked rhetorically, "What kind of clout can you have with manufacturers if you have 55 buyers?"

In the emerging world of electronic publishing, where industry structure has yet to solidify, some organizations have succeeded in the pursuit of cost economies based on scale while others have tossed in the towel. The New York Times' Books, Information, and Education Group falls into the latter category while Mead Corp.'s Data Central regards itself as one of the winners. In 1983, the Times' group concluded that it had had enough of electronic distribution, at least for the immediate future, having lost $3–4 million in this area between 1981 and 1982. Recognizing the group's limits, its vice president noted that "we don't bring anything unique to the distribution business. But we bring a lot to the business of collecting information." In effect, he was admitting that the Times had failed in its attempt to become a vertically integrated information services firm providing *both* the information or content *and* the information systems to store, process, and distribute it. The Times discovered that large capital investments in information systems, as well as experience obtainable only through years of operating electronic distribution facilities, were required before it could be a profitable participant in this industry.

When the Times exited, it gave its distribution business to Mead's Data Central, a company with a long track record in the field of electronic distribution, having successfully supported Lexis Mead's innovative database service for the legal profession. Independent firms like Lockheed's Dialog Information Services, which distributes over 120 data bases, and Data Central are able to amortize the cost of running their systems to a far greater extent than could the Times. Both independents achieved economies of scale, based on experience, specialization, and automation that gave them a distinct advantage over their less fortunate rivals.

COST: SCOPE

In 1975, economists John Panzer and Robert Willig coined the term *economies of scope* to describe cost savings that result from the scope of the firm's activities rather than from the scale of its operations. Roughly speaking, scope economies arise when it is less costly to combine the production of two or more product lines in a single firm than it would be to produce them separately.

More formally, firm F is said to enjoy the benefits of economies of scope with respect to product or products x/y (here x/y stands for either a single product with features x and y *or* for separate products x and y) and input i if F's total cost of producing x/y from i, $C_F(x/y, i)$, is less than firm A's cost of producing x from i, $C_A(x,i)$, plus firm B's cost of producing y from i, $C_B(y,i)$:

$$C_F(x/y, i) \text{ is less than } C_A(x,i) \text{ plus } C_B(y,i)$$

An economy of scope may develop, for example, when a given input (factor of production) cannot be divided but is only partially consumed or occupied and, hence, free for other uses. Or, it may appear when a single service is offered to replace previously separate services, provided the cost of the new is lower than the sum of the combined costs of the old. In this latter case, either the producer of the service or the consumer of it may be the beneficiary of a scope economy.

Economies of scope, we will see shortly, have a specific relevance in the information systems field. To sharpen the sense of this concept, consider the following examples of scope economies, based in general on sharable inputs:

By-product.   It is generally accepted that the cost of raising one flock of sheep for wool and another for mutton is more costly than raising one for both. The farmer who raises sheep for both purposes enjoys the benefits of scope economies.

Fixed factors.   If a passenger railroad is underutilized, use of the railroad for passengers *and* freight will provide economies of scope, all things being equal.

Reuse.   The firm that creates a general index of articles published in the sciences benefits from cost advantages due to scope economies when it reuses the general index to derive particular listings for sale to physicists, chemists, biologists, and the like.

Know-how.   A firm's know-how represents a shared input that may be used in producing a variety of products. If the firm can find ways to transfer proprietary knowledge or experience from its various activities at low costs, it may be able to enjoy the benefits of scope economies. On the open market, firms attempting to obtain proprietary knowledge face high acquisition costs.

Combinations.   The cost of manufacturing an AM/FM clock radio, by all reports, is less than producing *separately* an AM radio, an FM radio, and a clock, all things being equal.

Sears, Roebuck & Company takes advantage of scope economies based on know-how and a fixed factor of production to pursue its objective of providing customers with a full line of financial services. A Sear's spokesman says that by virtue of its size, the company has considerable technological know-how in data processing and telecommunications and intends to develop and market this capability.

In 1983, Sears negotiated an agreement with the Mellon Bank to process retail remittances for certain customers of the bank. In

1984, it arranged a test with the Phillips Petroleum Company to process credit card transactions involving 28 service stations and 12 stores in Oklahoma. Using its excess telecommunications and computer capacity, Sears developed an information system to authorize and record credit card transactions at the stations and stores. Upon completion of these steps, it transmits the data to a Phillips computer center for further processing.

Japan Airlines flies a similar economy-of-scope route when it finds fee-generating applications for its underutilized worldwide computer-based reservation system. Instead of using it exclusively for its original purpose, seat reservations on JAL flights, the airline now employs it to book tickets around the world for sports events, concerts, plays, and the like. Commenting on the scope economy, a JAL official said, "Why can't we buy Wimbleton tickets for our passengers who are flying to London and dream of watching the matches?"

From satisfying the dreams of JAL passengers to responding to the desires of hog farmers and cattle ranchers, economies of scope based on information systems are playing an increasingly important role. The farmers, it seems, would rather hear about changes in sow mating behavior due to variations in barn illumination than the newest strain of alfalfa and its effect on the portliness of calves. The ranchers, need it be said, have just the opposite preferences. To meet the needs of its multiple readerships, *Farm Journal* (the largest farm publication in the United States) publishes 1,134 different versions for its over 1 million subscribers.

Farm Journal divides its target audience into five major producer categories: cotton, dairy, beef, hogs, and livestock—and partitions the United States into 26 regions. For each of the 14 issues that an $8 annual subscription brings, about 20 percent of the editorial content remains the same in all versions. The rest combines 32 supplements, depending on the subscriber's profile.

The journal realized this opportunity to exploit scope economies based on the reuse of material when it switched to a new computer-controlled system offered by its printer, R. R. Donnelley & Sons in Chicago. Capitalizing on the new technology, *Farm Journal* can print, for example, 150,000 beef-only copies, 7,000 beef and dairy copies, and 25 copies for top producers of cotton, hogs, and dairy cows. Without this system, the journal could not afford to meet the increasingly specialized needs of its readers. Unlike subscribers to *The New Yorker* or *Reader's Digest*, "a farmer," according to *Farm Journal's* president, "doesn't pick up a farm magazine to be entertained."

Leaving the farm and moving to the factory, we encounter another form of scope economy, flexible manufacturing. By integrating information systems, robotics, and other forms of automation, firms like Deere no longer find themselves limited to particular product lines rigidly determined by highly specialized manufacturing equipment. In the flexible factory, firms can produce custom-made products in low volume at a profit. To duplicate this in a conventional factory would require several different assembly lines, each with its own costly set of machinery and specialized human resources.

In the Deere plant in Waterloo, Iowa, for example, tractors in more than 5,000 different configurations are produced for farmers desiring not only specialized publications but also custom designs. Deere saves on direct labor costs, since numerically controlled (NC) machines have replaced highly paid machinists. NC machines also lower the costs of retooling and finished-parts inventory. More significantly, the company can reprogram its machines for entirely different purposes. A Deere manager notes that "we can make aircraft parts or washing machine parts or almost anything within a certain size range." Racing to exploit its scope advantages, Deere formed a group to seek opportunities in defense and other nonfarm business areas.

Petroleum companies like Exxon, Texaco, and ARCO pioneered the development of sophisticated information systems to analyze geological data generated by satellite reconnaissance, seismic probes, and the like. To further refine their search for oil and gas formations, these companies compile extensive geological data bases. As a result, they have acquired unparalleled expertise and knowledge in a highly specialized field.

This technological knowledge, the oil giants discovered, is not limited to locating oil. It can be used by their geologists to help in the search for coal, uranium, and oil shale. For these alternative energy sources lie buried in sediment formations similar to those bearing oil and gas. When such crude-oil producers pursue these new veins, they benefit from scope economies based on their information systems know-how. Some economists have even suggested that scope economies, together with considerations such as managerial discretion and the regulatory climate, may have fueled diversification moves in the 70s by oil firms into the coal, uranium, and oil shale industries.

Information system know-how enabled Citibank to develop, as a by-product of its massive credit card–processing activities, a new service for retailers. With over 15 million Visa, Master, Diners and Carte Blanche cardholders, Citibank processes vast pools of transaction data. Pumping from these inexhaustible reservoirs, it created a series of marketing reports on customers for retailers intent on improving their merchandising, promotion, and advertising operations. These reports present summary statistics on buying patterns, customer groups, local demographics, and so on. The cost of creating this information on the outside would be prohibitive. Scope economies make it possible for Citibank and, by the way, for others similarly situated on top of valuable, essentially untapped data bases.

As a final, double-entry scope economy, consider the cost savings associated with automatic teller machines. For banks, ATMs clearly cut labor costs for routine transactions like deposits and withdrawals. But more importantly, just as flexible manufacturing enables innovators like Deere to offer a variety of products and lines, ATMs provide enterprising banks like Citibank, Banc One, and others, with an opportunity to create new fee-generating financial services based on scope economies obtained through combinations of previously discrete services or of entirely new ones. Bill payment, money market fund transfers, discount brokerage, and cash management accounts are all available—if not today, then tomorrow—on your bank's ATM network.

But it is not only the banks that enjoy the rewards of scope economies gained by combining services. Customers, too, benefit. Under the assumption that time is money, customer transaction costs can be substantially reduced when multiple financial services are obtained at an ATM. In the future, "home banking" will offer the same kind of scope economies.

COST: INFORMATION

Information economies enable relatively knowledgeable firms to acquire, produce, process, store, ship, or sell products at lower average cost per unit than relatively ignorant ones. Opportunities to benefit from economies of information may be found in each of the firm's functional areas. Like economies of scale and scope, economies of information have a price, which must be paid before the information advantage can be gained.

The sources of information economies run the gamut from intelligence on the costs, prices, and policies of the firm's strategic targets to data on economic, social, political, and technological trends affecting its products. Consider, for example, the cost reduction or avoidance opportunities arising from the organization's knowledge of such items as:

1. The costs and benefits of matching a competitor's promotional campaign wherever it is launched.
2. A competitor's advertising, credit, or pricing policies.
3. The prices charged by independent vendors who deal separately with the firm's local purchasing agents across the country.
4. The rules suppliers use to estimate, calculate, or otherwise determine the price you will pay for their product.

For each of these items, and countless others as well, knowledge could lead to advantage by enabling the firm to achieve economies of information. Not in all cases, of course. But there seem to be a sufficiently large number of possibilities—caused in many instances by opportunistic behavior on the part of the firm's suppliers, customers, or competitors—to make investments in the appropriate resources worthwhile to acquire such knowledge.

For example, Qantas, the Australian airline, suspected that its insurance premiums were too high. It checked by developing an information system to model three types of risk—accidents in the air, on the ground, and to passengers—and their costs. By comparing what was paid to what the model said should be paid, Qantas accountants confirmed their suspicions. Armed with this information, they renegotiated with the insurer and obtained lower rates. While insurers must protect themselves against customers who fail to disclose risk-related facts, clients, in turn, need to defend themselves against opportunistic insurance companies preying on the ignorant.

Equitable Life Assurance, the nation's third largest insurer, developed an on-line inventory control and purchasing system to tie the firm's field offices with its seven regional offices, four warehouses, and corporate headquarters in New York City. The warehouses stock paper clips, stationery, and other office supplies.

In the past, purchasing agents at the warehouses often lacked information to analyze vendor bids and determine the best buy. With the new system, Equitable corporate now purchases supplies from a distributor in New York and offers them to the warehouses at a bit above cost. The purchasing agents are free to buy from corporate or go outside. The system gives agents leverage during vendor negotiations, since they can access the system's data base to learn the terms of recent deals for items they want.

This strategic information system (SIS) enabled Equitable to reduce the bargaining power of its office-item suppliers. The system saves Equitable over $2 million a year, according to company sources.

While Equitable protects itself against vendors hawking goods, other organizations aim their information systems at those selling services. Xerox, Digital Equipment, and General Motors among others—all concerned about rising business travel expenses, estimated as the third largest controllable cost of doing business (after salaries and the cost of computers and related equipment)—have taken steps to reduce their costs in this area. New policies, backed by applications designed to aid in travel planning *and* to monitor travel expenses, give them an information advantage when negotiating corporate discounts with hotels, airlines, and car rental agencies, and encourage employees to comply with organizational guidelines. Systems report to management, for example, on whether employees take advantage of the lowest fares and rates available to the firm. This tends to have a dampening effect on those employees whose tastes do not match the corporate pocketbook or culture.

The rising costs of telephone services have prompted many organizations to defend themselves by becoming more knowledgeable, through the use of information systems, about calling and circuit activity. Sometimes, the mere distribution of a report detailing data on the time, type of call, number dialed, location, direction, cost, and account number to department heads causes impressive reductions in telephone expense. A Connecticut manufacturer found that such distribution reduced (in one of its departments) nonbusiness-related calls by 50 percent and the total monthly phone bill by $4,500. Such systems can also be employed to prevent blatant misuse, such as frequent calls to dial-a-joke, the weather or time, dial-a-porn messages, and the like. The state of Washington claims that it saved over $300,000 annually by programming its system to block such calls.

In addition to reducing telephone service expense vis-à-vis providers, some organizations use information systems to stem losses vis-à-vis clients or customers. A Chicago law firm recovers about $2,500 a month in hourly charges after examining printouts highlighting clients that its attorneys had not billed for time spent telephoning on their behalf.

Avoiding costs induced by the behavior of opportunistic customers motivates many to develop inventive applications designed to reduce such abuses. In the parking lot business, Edison Parking spent four years devising a system to prevent the loss of up to 20 percent in revenues due to customers who park illegitimately. Now customers must use a plastic identification card before gaining admittance to the lot. They insert the card into an optical reader linked to a central processing unit. The computer checks the validity of the account number, whether last month's bill has been paid, and so on. The garage door opens only if the card passes all tests.

To prevent "customers" who abuse refund policies from continuing their activities, a group of New York City department stores—Bloomingdale's, Gimbel's, and others—banded together, with the aid of an information system, to reduce their losses. What caused this rare act of solidarity were mounting losses due to fraudulent returns. These large retailers were being taken by a varied group of abusers:

- Shoplifters who remove sales tags and ask for refunds at the checkout counter.
- Models who purchase clothes, wear them for a shooting session, and then return them.
- Employees with discount privileges who buy merchandise at discounts and have friends return the items for cash at the regular price.

To meet the challenge posed by these individuals, the stores channeled all refunds through a single information system. In this way, the special customers could be identified by inspecting frequency-of-return reports generated by the system. By warning letters and the threat of more serious actions, the stores were able to stem their losses.

Another interesting game played between a business and its customers occurs most baldly at Atlantic City gambling casinos. To lure its best customers—the high rollers (i.e., those having the greatest probability of losing the most)—Caesar's Palace, Bally's, Harrah's, and other houses offer a well-orchestrated array of complimentary enticements ranging from free drinks, food, and room accomodations to transportation via private jet.

The object of the game, from the casinos' point of view, is to maximize the spread between the high roller's losses and the amount spent on the complimentaries tailored to the desires of the individual. To improve its chances of winning, casinos keep elaborate customer records on game preferences, betting patterns, favorite drinks, restaurants, entertainers, and so on. Not content only with the advantage guaranteed by the odds at the gambling table, casinos employ information systems to help improve their chances of selecting precisely those players who will yield the most net to the house. For gaming marketers, the opportunities are limitless. Yet, there are also risks. By designing an expensive package of complimentaries for a gambler, the house will lose if the player doesn't play as expected. To prevent this possibility, the casinos attempt to refine their analyses of the best prospects and weed out those who don't play by the "rules."

From information systems intended to get the upper hand in buyer relations, we turn now to a few designed to help customers reduce their expenses and, in the process, advance the interests of the system supplier. To support a cost reduction thrust in the customer arena (in contrast to Equitable's cost reduction thrust described above vis-à-vis its suppliers), the Hartford Insurance Company provides customers who have complex exposures and multiple claims with a computer-generated loss control analysis. Breaking out losses by location, time of day, type of accident, and so on, this information system pinpoints accident causes and, after preventive measures are taken, can lead to substantially lower premium costs for customers and more business for Hartford.

To help its customers improve their operations, Packaging Corporation of America, a large paperboard supplier, offers a host of specialized services. Knickerbocker Toys, one of PCA's customers, certainly was grateful for the assistance it received when it confronted a complex and costly packaging puzzle. Knickerbocker ships over 22 million individual items each year, with each toy requiring a different display carton, and each primary package a corrugated shipping container. It was the latter that caused the problem. For each primary package needed its own customized corrugated container. Before PCA offered its assistance, Knickerbocker juggled nearly 400 containers of varying sizes and shapes.

PCA's marketing services group designed an information system to solve Knickerbocker's puzzle. This enabled the toy company to cut its warehouse space by 50 percent and to reduce container setup costs by 75 percent. Moreover, with larger-volume container orders, the firm now enjoys substantial savings in unit costs. In helping Knickerbocker better manage its costs, PCA gained the respect and confidence of its customer, an important factor in the commoditylike packaging business.

Strategic information systems may also be used to secure an edge with more than one target or to support activities in one arena so that advantage may be gained in another. The manager of General Electric's distribution center for large appliances in Kentucky uses an application to help GE keep down its substantial shipping costs so that its retailers can maintain competitive prices. Xerox, Pratt & Whitney, General Motors, and others require their suppliers to provide computer-generated data on product quality, inventory levels, and the like, for the goods they supply. The desire to produce more efficiently rather than to gain advantage over suppliers motivates such initiatives. These new information-based demands, however, open competitive advantage opportunities for suppliers: As large customers formulate supplier plans in response to more intense competition, their strategies often aim at reducing the number of suppliers to a select few who can provide not only the desired components but also value-added services like computer-generated quality control reports. In this environment, a supplier's information system expertise can create a decisive edge in securing long-term contracts, which could preempt the business from competitors.

The use of information systems offensively against competitors is illustrated by some of the extensions of the airline reservation systems mentioned in Chapter 1. For example, the new cut-rate airlines contend that American and United use traffic information obtained from their systems to overcharge them just for being listed. Airlines without their own systems complain that the intricacies of Sabre and Apollo often stymie attempts to create innovative packages. As one rival put it, "If you're out of sync with their reservation system, then whatever you're doing won't exist." Finally, Braniff and Continental have argued that their recent cash flow problems are due in part to these automated reservation systems: When multiple carriers are involved, the first carrier in the itinerary is considered the ticketing airline, so it collects all the revenues, but repays the others only when the flight is over. That is, American and United are floating, while Braniff and Continental are sinking.

Economies of information, of course, are not limited to the profit sector. Government agencies have strategic targets also, and some of the latter have, on occasion, tried to beat the system. Recently, however, agencies have started to fight back, aiming computer-based weapons at those seeking to collect benefits they are not entitled to. Several examples follow.

Massachusetts saved $56 million in 1983 by automating its $1.2 billion Medicaid budget, formerly monitored by staff members adept at index card manipulation. The economies achieved were not due to personnel reductions. Rather, the state discovered that doctors, hospitals, and others were overbilling it.

California devised a system in 1978 to eliminate jobless-benefit payments to those attempting to rip off the state through the "fictitious-employer scheme." The scheme works like this: The thieves set up a phony business, pay some unemployment insurance taxes for fictitious employees, lay them off (so to speak), and then collect jobless benefits by posing as laid-off employees. This fraud certainly isn't limited to the inventiveness of Californians. A New Yorker formed 28 corporations, created 168 aliases, and collected $600,000 before he was caught. Through the use of information systems modeled after California's, states have significantly reduced their losses in this area.

The Boston-State Retirement Board knew something was amiss when it, after asking its 14,500 pension recipients to submit proof that they were still among the living, received responses from 13,994. Inspired by this saving of over $700,000 from the $85 million it pays each year, the board contracted with Hooper Holmes, a company that supplies continuously updated magnetic tape listings of the social security numbers of some 12 million deceased persons. With these listings, the Board has written a program to detect those illicit claimants from another world.

Since 1981, New York City's Tax Division has run a computerized program to catch evaders of city taxes. At the end of 1983, it had aided in the collection of more than $40 million from over 55,000 individuals and businesses. By simple file-matching procedures, the division identified those who failed to pay taxes on commercial rent, business income, and personal income.

CASE REFERENCES

American Air   See Case References, Chapter 1.

American Medical International   *Business Week*, November 7, 1983; *The Wall Street Journal*, October 29, 1983.

ARCO   Teece, "Economies of Scope and the Scope of the Enterprise" (see Bibliography to this chapter).

Bally's   *Business Week*, July 30, 1984.

Bloomingdale's   *Chain Store Age Executive*, May 1982.

Boston   *Computerworld*, January 17, 1983.

Braniff Air   See **American Air.**

Caesar's Palace   *ICP Interface*, Summer 1982; see **Bally's.**

California   *The Wall Street Journal*, July 20, 1983.

Chase Manhattan   *New York Times*, January 28, 1982.

Citibank   *The Wall Street Journal*, March 29, 1984; May 4, 1984.

Chicago Law Firm   See **Connecticut Manufacturer.**

Connecticut Manufacturer   *The Office*, April 1982.

Continental Air   See **American Air.**

Deere   *New York Times*, December 18, 1983.

R. R. Donnelley   See **Citibank** and *Farm Journal.*

Edison Parking   *Computerworld*, November 21, 1983.

Equitable Life   *Computerworld*, May 10, 1982.

Exxon   See **ARCO.**

Foster & Marshall   See **Shearson/American Express.**

Farm Journal   *The Wall Street Journal*, January 21, 1983.

First National Bank of Chicago   See **Chase Manhattan.**

GE   *The Wall Street Journal*, December 31, 1981.

General Bancshares   *The Wall Street Journal*, December 12, 1983.

Gimbel's   See Bloomingdale's.

GM   *The Wall Street Journal*, September 20, 1983.

Hartford Insurance   *New York Times*, advertisement.

Harrah's   See Bally's.

Humana   *Business Week*, January 9, 1984; *New York Times*, May 8, 1983.

Japan Air   *The Wall Street Journal*, February 17, 1984.

Knickerbocker Toys   See Packaging Corporation of America.

Levitz   *Business Week*, February 7, 1983.

Lifemark   See American Medical International.

Massachusetts   *The Wall Street Journal*, November 27, 1984; *Information Systems News*, November 27, 1984.

Mead Data   *Business Week*, March 7, 1983; *New York Times*, April 23, 1984.

Mellon Bank   See Sears.

New York City   *Computerworld*, January 9, 1984.

New York Times   See Mead Data.

Phillips Petroleum   See Sears.

Packaging Corporation of America   *Paperboard Packaging*, August 1982.

Qantas Air   *ICP Interface*, Autumn 1982.

Sears, Roebuck   *The Wall Street Journal*, May 17, 1983; February 10, 1984; April 25, 1984.

Shearson/American Express   *The Wall Street Journal*, January 8, 1982.

Telephone Information Systems   See Connecticut Manufacturer.

Texaco   See ARCO.

Washington   *The Wall Street Journal*, April 11, 1984.

Xerox   *Business Week*, August 22, 1983; *The Wall Street Journal*, July 30, 1982.

BIBLIOGRAPHY

Bailey, Elizabeth E., and Ann F. Friedlaender. "Market Structure and Multiproduct Industries." *Journal of Economic Literature*, September 1982.

Hayes, Robert H., and Stephen C. Wheelwright. *Restoring Our Competitive Edge: Competing through Manufacturing*. New York: John Wiley & Sons, 1984.

Leibenstein, Harvey. *Beyond Economic Man: A New Foundation for Microeconomics*. Cambridge, Mass.: Harvard University Press, 1980.

Panzar, John C., and Robert W. Willig. "Economies of Scale and Economies of Scope in Multioutput Production." *Bell Labs Economic Discussion Paper* 33, 1975.

Robinson, E. A. G. *The Structure of Competitive Industry*. 2d ed. Chicago: University of Chicago Press, 1958.

Scherer, F. M. *Industrial Market Structure and Economic Performance*. 2d ed. Skokie, Ill.: Rand McNally, 1980.

Shepherd, William G. *The Economics of Industrial Organization*. Englewood Cliffs, N.J.: Prentice-Hall, 1979.

Teece, David J. "Economics of Scope and the Scope of the Enterprise." *Journal of Economic Behavior and Organization* 1, no. 1 (1980).

Williamson, Oliver E. *Markets and Hierarchies: Analysis and Antitrust Implications*. New York: Free Press, 1975.

5

Innovation

KINDS OF INNOVATION

In 1959, when Xerox introduced its first copier, the 914, it realized the dream of Chester Carlson, the patent attorney who conceived the basic idea 20 years earlier. The 914 product was an innovation, invented by Carlson and imitated (in one form or another, in due course) by a long line of competitors who entered the industry Xerox created.

While it took Xerox two decades to bring Carlson's idea to market, Dr. L. A. B. Pilkington saw his dream become reality in just seven years. In 1954, he thought of a new way to make plate glass, then manufactured by grinding the surface of a continuous glass ribbon until the desired thickness and quality were reached. To replace this rather wasteful and costly process, Pilkington imagined an entirely different procedure, one that eliminated grinding altogether by floating a continuous feed of molten glass on a layer of molten tin.

Invented by Pilkington and developed by Pilkington Brothers Ltd., a British glass manufacturer, the float-glass process was an industry-transforming innovation, making this relatively small firm a leading player. Shortly after its commercial introduction in 1961, the process was licensed to Pittsburgh Plate Glass in the United States and to St. Gobains in France. Within a few years, all major producers, under agreements with Pilkington, manufactured plate glass by the float process, which enabled them to reduce production cost substantially.

Innovation, as these examples show, includes the adoption of new products or processes. A product innovation satisfies customer needs or wants previously unmet. A process innovation improves the efficiency or effectiveness of a process associated with a product. An innovation may relate to one or more links on the product (industry, value-added) chain, which typically covers: product and process R&D, purchase and transportation of raw materials, manufacturing of parts and components, assembly, testing and quality control, marketing, sales, wholesale distribution, and retailing. It may stem from technological, organizational, or other sources.

Innovation is the middle stage in the sequence that starts with invention (creation) and ends with imitation (diffusion). *Invention* is the first confidence that something should work, "the stage at which the scent is first picked up." *Innovation* is the first commercial application of an invention, "the stage at which the hunt is in full cry," comprising such activities as refining the initial idea, prototyping, engineering and design, tooling, manufacturing setup and start-up, and marketing. Economists estimate that invention consumes 5–15 percent of the total cost of realizing new products or processes, while innovation takes the remainder. *Imitation*, the final stage, signals the success of the innovation.

The 914 copier and the float-glass process were major innovations. Other product and process changes may not have such far-reaching consequences. Yet these qualify as innovations if they bring into existence a new product that catches on or they alter (to a degree often difficult to determine) the established conduct of business in an industry. This implies that innovations may either be unprecedented (like the two just mentioned) or be new applications of concepts developed in other contexts.

While the boundary between a slight modification and a prior innovation may be difficult to perceive, we need not be troubled here by this failure of vision. For I am not so much concerned with drawing theoretical lines as with uncovering opportunities to use information systems strategically. To this end, we need to understand the various sources of product and process innovations, since these are the ingredients of innovative strategic thrusts.

Strategic innovation thrusts are strategic moves intended to increase the firm's competitive advantage or reduce the advantage(s) of its strategic targets. An innovation thrust can be defensively employed by a firm to imitate a competitor's innovation by introducing its own variant, not precisely the same as the pioneer's but different enough to be considered a minor innovation in its own right.

A firm may introduce a process innovation that simultaneously reduces cost and improves quality to such an extent that customers perceive its product as far superior to the competition's. Finally, like its close relatives, differentiation and cost, innovation often goes hand in hand with other thrusts.

INNOVATION: PRODUCT

Like most religious rituals, the process of identifying innovation opportunities remains a mystery, defying rational explanation. And their development is largely an act of faith, vision, and energy. Before Xerox launched the 914 copier, it commissioned three independent studies to determine market demand. Two major consulting firms reported that demand was so low the project ought to be scrapped. The third was more optimistic, projecting cumulative totals of 8,000 placements (maximum) and 3,000 (minimum) by the end of six years. Yet within three years after launch, 80,000 914s were in place.

Beyond the eternally black bowels of the earth from which revolutionary products like the Xerox 914 emerge as major innovations, lies a region of opportunity far more amenable to conceptual understanding. Assume for a moment that a product exists. Ask the question: What can I do to ensure the continued life of this product? Answers to this question, I suggest, will provide a rich source of product innovation ideas.

Begin by reviewing the main features of the current product. Can any be modified to create a new version? Can performance be improved? Can the product be put to other uses? Can it be enlarged? Miniaturized? Rearranged? Concatenated with other products? Second, ask customers about improvements they would like or problems they've encountered. Third, consider competitors' products. Can you differentiate your offering from theirs? Can you provide a new combination of product features and services? Answers to such questions may lead to a product innovation opportunity.

In 1977, Merrill Lynch, the largest U.S. brokerage house, announced a new product, the Cash Management Account (CMA), offering under one umbrella three appealing services to investors: credit through a standard margin account, cash withdrawal by check or Visa debit card, and automatic investment of cash, dividends, etc., in a Merrill-managed money market fund.

Hawked by its brokers to clients with minimum balances of $20,000, CMAs moved slowly during their first few years. Brokers couldn't see what was in it for them. Realizing this lack of incentive, Merrill dangled free trips to Hawaii and Puerto Rico as rewards for attracting the greatest number of CMAs. The troops responded by running CMAs up the exponential curve: 1980/ 180,000 accounts, 1981/560,000 accounts, 1982/900,000 accounts, 1983/over 1 million accounts.

These efforts brought in over 450,000 new accounts, accounts that had not been with the firm previously. Merrill reaps over $60 million a year in fees from the more than $20 billion it manages in the three money market funds associated with the CMA product.

The CMA is an innovative product, providing scope economies to customers as well as to Merrill. The product would never have left the launching pad without a 162-step (subsequently patented) computer program; the help of Banc One, a bank-holding company (see Chapter 1) that issues the CMA debit card and processes CMA checking and card transactions; and Merrill's resources in database and laser printing technology.

With this product-based strategic innovation thrust, made possible by information systems, Merrill preempted the market from a monopoly position for four years. Competition from other financial services organizations did not appear until 1981; and at the close of 1982, Merrill's closest rival, Dean Witter, had only 90,000 customers for its active asset account. Only in 1983 and thereafter did Merrill's premier position begin to erode as banks and other financial service organizations finally entered the market with similar products and the information systems technology needed to support them.

An enterprising market research firm, National Decision Systems of San Diego, captured another form of product innovation opportunity. The U.S. Constitution mandates a population count every 10 years to reapportion seats in the House of Representatives. Not content to tally only heads, the decennial census has developed over the years an insatiable appetite for data, from the basics of age, sex, and race to the number of holes drilled or dug (if your water comes from wells) and babies had (if you're a householder).

In 1980, the data collected by the Census Bureau filled 38 reels of computer tape. By 1983, the bureau had still not issued its report on the 226 million Americans who had completed questionnaires. But it offered to sell the raw results of this $1 billion survey sponsored by the American taxpayers to anyone willing to pay $38,000 for the tapes.

The purchaser could, for example, use them for its own purposes or merely package the tapes in attractive containers and advertise their availability. This would add some value, but not much; it certainly wouldn't count as an innovation. Or the purchaser might divide the data on the 38 reels into (say) 3,800 different categories and offer each for sale in diskette form suitable for microcomputer analysis. This, too, adds value to the raw data but wouldn't (except under the most liberal interpretation) be considered innovative, since the distributor's function of "breaking lots" is not something that ordinarily turns heads. But an illuminating transformation of the raw data through analysis and a presentation of the results in a readily available form should, I suggest, count as an innovation.

This is precisely what National Decisions did with the 1980 U.S. Census data. It purchased (at less than cost) a complete set of tapes and developed information systems to process the raw data and present it in attractive form. What National did, anyone with the requisite expertise could have done with this uncopyrighted material.

National added value to the raw computer tapes by preparing a five-volume compendium of the 1980 census, offering it for $395 as a set. It sells to those involved in market research, demographic analysis, and so on. It's a value-added product that could only be produced through the aid of information systems designed to analyze and report on the 1980 tracts. National Decisions saw an opportunity and pursued it. In this marketplace, National Decisions enjoys first-mover advantages.

The innovations of Merrill Lynch and National Decisions, while noteworthy, pale beside the achievement of Federal Express. In 1983, just 10 years after it got off the ground, this overnight, door-to-door delivery service of business goods and messages flew past the $1 billion revenue mark for the first time. Carrying 43 million packages, serving 550,000 customers in 40,000 communities across the United States, and still expanding domestically and internationally, FE represents a by-now legendary case of business innovation, innovation that depends essentially on the strategic use of information systems.

The company operates an armada of over 75 aircraft, a fleet of more than 5,000 delivery vans, and a central sorting facility, the hub, located in Memphis, Tennessee. Each day, couriers pick up shipments from senders and load them on planes bound for the hub. Most planes arrive between midnight and 1:00 A.M. After their cargoes are unloaded and sorted, they are reloaded to return to their points of origin carrying only shipments addressed to locations in these areas. Couriers at the destination points deliver priority packages by 10:30 A.M.

The hub-and-spoke idea, applied for the first time in 1973 by Fred Smith (the founder of FE) to the delivery of packages, transformed the rather sleepy airfreight business. The success of Smith's entrepreneurial venture depends on interrelated networks of ground, air, and electronic (computer and telecommunications) systems.

Consider, for example, how the ground and air networks are linked by the electronic network when a customer calls to request a pickup:

1.   The customer's call is switched automatically to one of FE's three centers, where a service representative receives it.

2.   The request is then transmitted to the Memphis computer system, where it is printed and displayed on a terminal screen.

3.   If the request is for a package in a major city, it is routed by FE's recently installed digitally aided dispatch system (Dads) to a courier (van driver) in the field. Dads consists of a small computer and a video display terminal attached to a digital radio in the van. It enables drivers to communicate with an FE dispatcher electronically linked to the hub computer. When a driver signs on to a mobile terminal, orders for the day are displayed on the screen.

4. After the courier picks up the package, he or she enters identifying data into the terminal so that a dispatcher can close out all requests at the end of the day.

5. Before the package is shipped, its airbill number is scanned electronically and transmitted via FE's satellite net to the Memphis computer. Frequent electronic monitoring is one of the features of FE's offering that differentiates it from the competition. For it enables customers who inquire about their shipment to determine its status along the way as well as the date and time of its delivery.

6. At each embarkation point and airport ramp, there is a computer terminal connected to FE's data network. By taking the pulse of its packages at various checkpoints along the shipment chain, FE can compute individual flight plans to accomodate variations from anticipated volumes. Such computer-generated plans also take into consideration weather conditions, traffic delays, rerouting of trucks to alternative airports, and the like.

7. Upon arrival at the hub, packages are sorted in FE's half-million–square-foot building along 17½ miles of automated, high-speed conveyor belts.

FE's innovative approach to the airfreight business has brought it about 50 percent of the market. Its success in the past and its plans for the future—geographical expansion both domestically and internationally and diversification into the electronic mail business with its Zap-mail service—depend heavily on its strategic use of information systems, an innovative, entrepreneurial use that has transformed the structure of the airfreight industry.

INNOVATION: PROCESS

Like preemptive strikes[15]—major moves made ahead of competitors, through which the firm secures an advantageous position by being the first mover and from which it is difficult to dislodge—opportunities for process innovation may occur up and down the constantly evolving industry chain. Indeed, many preemptive strikes are major process innovations related to manufacturing—Japanese

improvements in the production of 64k RAM chips; distribution—
BIC ballpoint pen and L'Eggs pantyhose sales in supermarkets, a
channel never used for such products previously; and so on.

The process innovator therefore must look systematically at
the chain of activities, goods, and services associated with the development, production, distribution, sale, financing, maintenance, etc., of a particular product. At one or more points, opportunities for an innovative strategic thrust might arise. Promising
sites to explore, which are illustrated by the cases to follow, include:

- *Resource identification/selection*: Opportunities to develop innovative procedures to identify or select resources critical to the
  development, manufacture, distribution, etc., of the product.
- *Distribution*: Opportunities to provide innovative distribution
  channels, services, and the like.
- *Retailing*: Opportunities to alter the normal procedures for retailing products, affecting both customers and suppliers.
- *Service processing*: Opportunities to provide a firm's service at
  substantially lower cost or higher quality because of processing
  innovations associated with it.

This list is not exhaustive. As usual, targets for possible innovative
strategic thrusts may be selected from among the firm's generic suppliers, customers, or competitors (see Chapter 2).

Suppose the basketball coach of the men's 1984 U.S. Olympic
team picked his players according to the following criteria:

Identification:	Height—at least 6'10".
	Weight—between 180 and 250 pounds.
	Scoring average—18 points/game.
	Team winning ratio—greater than .500.
Selection:	After observing identified prospects perform
	in practice games, decide intuitively.

Now, suppose the coach of the French team identified and selected prospects strictly in terms of their ability to pass an intricate series of speed, dexterity, and intelligence tests. As a result, the French team consists of 10 extremely quick, nimble, and bright players whose average height, it turns out, is 5'6" and whose basketball experience is one to three months. Against the U.S. team, it is safe to say, France would be at a competitive disadvantage. We know this immediately, the contest having been determined by the identification and selection criteria used by each coach.

This hypothetical case underlines the importance of identifying and selecting the right materials for the task at hand—the ingredients, as it were, of success. In sports, money management, and politics—to name but three areas in which this principle rules—enterprising organizations seek innovative strategic thrust opportunities to transform (to their advantage) traditional ways of identifying and selecting the ingredients of success. The examples to follow show how these may be supported or shaped by information systems.

Moving from the ridiculous to the sublime, consider the Dallas Cowboys, pro football's most successful team with (to date) 18 consecutive winning seasons, 12 division championships, and two Super Bowl victories in five appearances. When the Cowboys' franchise was created in 1960, president and general manager Tex Schramm had a vision about improving the player identification and selection process. He believed that through the use of computers (then applied in pro football, if at all, for the most mundane accounting and payroll functions), Dallas could gain a competitive edge. Together with a friend at IBM's Service Bureau Company, he initiated a project to define those player attributes, position by position, that made a good football player.

By 1965, after four years of research and development, a system for evaluating and selecting players was up and running. As experience with the system grew, being enriched by feedback on what particular factors led to success once a player was selected and playing on the team, management confidence in this new competitive weapon grew. It enabled the Cowboys to improve the accuracy of scouting reports, often biased by personal preferences for factors such as speed, or hitting power, by assigning weights based on past performance to each scout.

While it is impossible to determine the precise value of the Cowboys' strategic information system, the testimony of its vice president for player development (the principal user) serves as a reliable proxy.

> Today I am very excited about the system, and how we now can get the percentage a player has of playing in the league, what percentage he has of starting, and what are the most and least important qualities that make up a successful football player. When we started, we had a four-room house of grey vanilla—and it ended up a mansion . . . . Life is percentages. If we can arrive at a 52 percent possibility rather than 50 percent, we will be that much better off.[16]

Schramm echoes this sentiment in saying, "We have an *advantage* because we've been doing it the longest. Other teams take a simplistic approach and don't specifically rank players the way we do. They may use the computer more in terms of simply listing what players are available in which positions, and their size."

In pro football, advantage is determined in large part by the talent assembled on the field; in money management, by the investments in the portfolio. Expertise in the processes of identification and selection, while important in the former, are absolutely essential in the latter. For more conventional money managers, portfolio construction proceeds stock by stock. One learns the pros and cons of individual companies by visiting plants, assessing competitors and patterns of industry evolution, listening with a third ear to public relations announcements, and the like.

Not so with Batterymarch, the path-breaking money management firm from Boston led by Dean LeBaron, a contrarian. From 1970 to 1983, Batterymarch exceeded or matched the Standard & Poor's 500 Stock Index 12 times. The firm's 15 percent annual rate of return topped the market rate by 6 percent.

LeBaron's method for identifying and selecting investments prescribes two steps: (1) formulate a general investment strategy; and (2) use the computer to identify and select investments conforming to the dictates of the strategy.

Since its formation in 1970, Batterymarch has pursued 12 strategies, couched in such terms as:

- Invest in small to medium-sized companies selling at low price earnings ratios and owned by less than 10 percent of other money managers.
- Invest in companies with new plant and equipment, which have greater tax deductions (due to depreciation) and whose reported earning are therefore artificially low.
- Invest in companies with low ratios of price to sales value, as an inflation hedge and a bet that asset-rich companies might be taken over.

These investment strategies translate into computer programs written to search through 4,000 or so issues, make arcane calculations consistent with the guidelines, and ultimately identify and select all and only those stocks satisfying strategic criteria. Computers suggest and execute all trades at Batterymarch; only one technician monitors the system. This innovative strategic use of information systems catapulted Batterymarch in less than 15 years into the nation's 11th largest stock market investor, the sixth largest excluding banks, with over $11 billion in assets.

LeBaron's innovation transformed a critical industry process. Listen to what peers say about the changes wrought by Batterymarch.

"They're reinventing virtually every part of the investment process." (Charles Ellis, financial services consultant from Greenwich, Connecticut.)

"LeBaron has probably set the pace for large money managers in America. He has a *process* for managing large sums of money, which have historically been the downfall of money managers." (Roger Hertog, executive vice president at Sanford C. Bernstein & Co., a $2.3 billion money manager based in New York City.)

From the stadium and the trading room to the political ring, astute professionals gain an edge by using computer technology imaginatively. To complete this triad of examples illustrating strategic innovation thrusts related to sports, money, and politics, we turn to the role played by systems in fundamentally transforming aspects of the American political scene.

The Republican Party pioneered in the application of computers to the processes of identifying and selecting contributors. Traditionally, Republicans paid their bills by digging into the pockets of a small group of wealthy individuals. Democrats, on the other hand, covered their costs from the nickels and dimes contributed by the masses. At least that's how the story used to run. But now, after applying the fruits of information processing technology to support its fund-raising campaigns, the Republicans claim that over 70 percent of their National Committee's revenues come from contributions of less than $25.

Even the Democrats agree that the Republicans have established a major competitive advantage in this area. The former executive director of the Democratic National Committee believes that:

> The various wings of the national Republican apparatus are now raising at least 10 times more money than the various segments of the Democratic National Committee. Now, when you include the money raised by the Republican and Democratic candidates, the spread is considerably less, but there is a threshold, a financial critical mass, which the Republicans already have and the Democrats have not.[17]

The Democrats appreciate the bind their strategic information systems blindness imposes upon them. "We saw the result in 1981 when the Republicans harvested the product of a decade of systematic and disciplined investment in the new technology: A Reagan presidency, a Republican-led Senate, and a working Republican minority in the House."

The Republicans seized the opportunity to use information systems to gain an edge. They now reap the rewards of their strategic vision, while the Democrats play catch-up. Recently, the Democratic Party appointed a director of management information systems to lead its national efforts in this area. He views his function as corresponding "to the role of an MIS organization in a decentralized company, where it sets standards and provides services without dictating policy." Contrast this perspective on information systems with the one held by his counterpart, the head of the Republican's Computer Services Division: "My job is to do not only what management of the committee would like done but to guide them as to what is possible." The latter, it seems, reflects a strategic perspective on information systems. The former, as his title indicates, still seems mired in the conventional.

In the 1984 elections, the Republicans moved beyond the use of information systems to identify potential contributors. Their innovations now extend to three other critical areas in which information systems are used to identify:

1. Unregistered voters likely to support Republican candidates, and take steps to get them enrolled. The Republican National Hispanic Assembly, an arm of the Republican National Committee, used an assortment of lists to generate the names of "upwardly mobile Hispanics," according to the group's executive director.

2. Potential Republican voters who might be away from their residence on election day. Members of this group are then sent applications for absentee ballots.

3. Voter concerns on a day-to-day basis in every state. The results of such poll watching enable Republican candidates to fine-tune their messages and arrange their promotions and advertising accordingly.

In the health care industry, the innovations of American Hospital Supply are, by now, classic exemplars of the strategic use of information systems. The company manufactures, markets, and distributes health care products to hospitals, laboratories, and medical specialists worldwide. In 1976, it introduced a computerized order-entry system, dubbed ASAP (American's analytical systems automated purchasing system), for customer use. Using an ASAP terminal, hospital staff members place orders directly for any of American's full line of over 100,000 products. By 1984, over 4,200 customers were tied to American electronically via ASAP.

If American lost access to ASAP for a period of only five days, according to a senior executive at the firm, the consequences would be dire: loss of market share and control of its business. To protect itself from the loss of so integral a part of its operations, American established a backup site capable of handling all ASAP transactions and normal company processing.

As American tells it, ASAP "helps customers by simplifying the ordering process and permitting customers to reduce their inventories." American consultants are available to assist customers in learning to use ASAP, "improve the hospital's purchasing procedures, reduce on-hand inventory, standardize their use of supplies, and implement improved patient-change procedures." With newer versions of ASAP, the purchasing process can be reduced to only one manual step—approving the order. Everything else is linked by ASAP to the hospital's computer system and by high-speed telephone lines to American's processing facilities and through them to over 122 distribution centers nationwide.

Now listen to what the competition has to say about ASAP, to get a better sense of the strategic significance of one of the first uses of an information system as a competitive weapon. Industry executives claim that "ASAP was largely responsible for driving competitors like A. S. Aloe Company and Will Ross Inc. from the national hospital supply distribution business. Once a hospital got an ASAP terminal, American couldn't be budged." As a director at rival United Hospital Supply puts it, "There will never be another American Hospital Supply. Who's kidding who? It's almost impossible for a hospital to avoid doing business with them." One former employee says its like having the fox in the hen house, but admits that American saves its customers' money also.

In our terms, American launched a preemptive strike in 1976, and it succeeded. The ASAP project represents an innovative strategic thrust that transformed a basic link on the industry chain—order entry—and in the process, raised customer switching costs. American captured an opportunity for using information systems to win an enduring competitive advantage.

In the news business, the recent innovation by Reuters also marks a strategic thrust backed by information systems. In 1851, Baron de Reuter had an idea. He believed that news of stock transactions on the Brussels exchange could be sold if distributed with dispatch. With the aid of carrier pigeons, he made this idea a reality and, in the process, founded the Reuters News Service. Over the years, ownership passed from the Reuter family to a primarily British consortium of press groups: the Newspaper Publishing Association, a Fleet Street trade group (41 percent share); the Press Association, a wire service owned by provincial English newspapers (41 percent share); the Australian and New Zealand press associations (16.4 percent share); and Reuter's management (1.4 percent share).

In 1984, the private consortium decided to put 28 percent of Reuters up for sale. The news agency known to millions for its stories from around the world was valued at about $370 million when its stock was publicly offered. What few realized, however, was that the bulk of Reuter's revenue derived not from general news stories but from reporting and processing of financial data in the world's financial capitals. Reuter's recent growth has been nothing short of spectacular, with revenue climbing from $125 million in 1980 to $254 million in 1981 to $337 million in 1983, and with pretax profit soaring from $2.7 million in 1980 to $30 million in 1981 and $43.5 million in 1983. Reliable estimates put about 85 percent of revenue and between 95 and 100 percent of profit in the financial information sector of its business. To achieve these heights, Reuters needed to rely on more than the undisputed talents of its carrier pigeons.

Among the first (unlike its traditional competitors, the Associated Press and the financially troubled United Press International) to realize that information systems are the wings of the 80s, Reuters fashioned an innovative strategic thrust in the early 70s to redefine its business. The thrust called for the development of computerized information and retrieval systems targeted at banks, stock and commodity traders, and other businesses. The systems would provide the latest prices from stock, bond, money, oil, commodity, and other international markets. Additional economic services would be added as the business evolved. At the heart of the system would be the Reuter's monitor, a video screen and keyboard to give immediate access to financial and general news data bases.

As the following statistics show, Reuters successfully implemented its strategic program: 15,000 subscribers, more than 32,500 Reuter's monitors in use, and 6,500 teleprinters displaying everything from currency prices to oil tanker rentals. Reuter's customers in the currency market, for example, can now not only call up the latest transactions for viewing but also link directly to dealers for trading. The introduction of this financial exchange service and the recent launch of a similar service for bonds make Reuters the dominant force in modern trading operations. It also provides a locked-in client base for other products. By creating one of the few financial information distribution and processing channels, Reuters, like American Hospital Supply and others with SIS vision, captured a preemptive position, a position based on the innovative use of computer technology.

From resource identification/selection and distribution, we move now to retailing. As one of the major processes in the consumer product chain, it comprises all the activities involved in selling goods or services directly to customers for personal, nonbusiness use. When an organization—be it a manufacturer, wholesaler, supermarket, department, or speciality store—engages in this kind of selling, it is retailing. Retailers may ply their trade in a store, on the sidewalk, at a concert. Products may be sold in person, over the telephone, through vending machines; it's all retailing.

Ever since the establishment of Bon Marchí, the first department store, retailing has witnessed one innovation after another, from mail order to catalog showroom, from gas station convenience store to community shopping center. Two recent examples are of interest to us because they use information systems to support or shape strategic innovation thrusts.

Founded in the early 70s, Comp–U–Card International turned a profit for the first time in 1983. Its original business provided a telephone-based service to shoppers who wanted to compare prices of brand name products across the country. By paying an annual membership fee of $25, a shopper could call a CUC representative, ask for the price of an item, and if acceptable, place an order. CUC, having neither inventory nor warehouse, would forward the order to the manufacturer, distributor, or other intermediary offering the product at the price the consumer had agreed to pay. In effect, CUC acted as the shopper's agent. As such, it received a small percentage of each sale. But this wasn't its main source of revenue. That came from fees paid by over 1 million CUC members.

The original CUC service kept tabs on products manually. In 1979, CUC automated its data base of over 60,000 items and launched the first interactive home computer shopping service, a strategic innovation thrust shaped by information systems. CUC markets this service, called Comp–U–Store, itself and through the Source, Dow Jones, and CompuServe information services to members with micros and modems.

The Comp–U–Store innovation led in 1984 to Comp–U–Mall, a browsing service for subscribers who wish to explore CUC's name brand items or stroll electronically through a mall whose "stores" offer such lines as discount drugs, flowers, and speciality items from Neiman-Marcus.

Is there an alternative to conventional supermarket shopping? In West Los Angeles, the answer is yes. The Phone In–Drive Thru Market offers shoppers an opportunity to call in orders for over 4,000 grocery and general merchandise items (each having a five-digit code) appearing in a bimonthly catalog. The listing includes national brands and generics if available. Currently, operators take the orders and enter them on computer terminals. At this point, the Phone In–Drive Thru information system takes over.

The system batches orders, analyzes them, and generates a bulk pick list and an optimal route for employees wheeling large carts through the Phone In–Drive Thru warehouse. Exhibiting a modicum of intelligence not always found at supermarket check-out counters, the system determines packing sequences that place, for instance, canned goods at the bottom of the bag and bread, grapes, and potato chips on top.

When customers arrive to pick up their orders, they first stop at a terminal station that displays instructions. After they enter their IDs, the screen lists the items ordered and prices. The customer writes a personal check (approved in advance) and drives to a des-ignated pickup lane (the place where the computer has instructed the picker to leave the order), receives the order, pays, and departs, usually having spent about four minutes at the market.

This innovative retailing operation, the brainchild of a computer consultant to the Jewel Food Stores in Chicago (one of the leading users of information systems among supermarket chains) and an entrepreneur who founded the Malibu Grand Prix amusement center, plans to expand over the next two years by opening 16 additional markets, mostly in the West. Prime targets are upscale suburbs and Snow Belt cities. At these new outlets, customers with push-button phones will be able to key in their orders automatically. Eventually, of course, the chain plans to accomodate shoppers with home computers.

Innovative retail services like the ones introduced by Comp-U-Card and Phone In–Drive Thru upset normal expectations and relationships up and down the product chain. In the case of CUC, price competition among vendors increases; for Phone In, vendors that depend on impulse sales tied to attractive or unusual packaging will have to think of new gimmicks.

In the home-buying market, the traditional process of financing the sale is undergoing a radical change. High interest rates, the secondary market for mortgages, and deregulation in the financial services industry account for some but not all of it. Technological advances in information processing and telecommunications need to be factored in as well.

Until the early 80s, the purchase of a home had been largely a local affair involving buyer, broker, and banker. The broker, familiar with the available properties, would show them to the prospective buyer. To finance the sale, the buyer would arrange a mortgage with the neighborhood savings and loan or bank, which financed it from the deposits of local customers.

First Boston, an entrepreneurial investment banking house, detected an opportunity to disrupt this long-standing menage à trois. It designed a computer-based mortgage network to put buyers and lenders together directly, in many cases bypassing the local banker. Called Shelternet, the system allows a prospective home buyer to apply for a mortgage through a real estate broker and receive a conditional commitment for a loan in less than an hour. According to a First Boston representative, "You can take an application, do an appraisal, do the follow-up work, and clear the loan inside of three weeks, whereas in California right now, it is taking anywhere from 60 to 90 days for a bank to process a mortgage."

First Boston wrote the software for Shelternet in-house. It is offered to brokers as part of a package that includes an IBM personal computer, installation, and the cost of establishing a separate mortgage service company, which is considered a necessity if currently unlicensed brokers hope to be certified as mortgage originators. Most prospective Shelternet clients are large, metropolitan realtors with no mortgage banking experience. First Boston also offers Shelternet to banks that cannot (because of interstate banking laws prohibiting such moves) open branches across the country but which can offer mortgage loans anywhere. After nine months of operation, the system generated $14 billion worth of mortgages.

As expected, some mortgage bankers have not looked too kindly at this innovation. According to the president of the Mortgage Bankers Association of America, "At least a segment of the mortgage banking community thinks that we're not yet ready for a nationwide mortgage information system. They view it as a substitute for the close, interpersonal relationships so crucial between lenders and home buyers."

In the energy management business, Honeywell and Johnson Control share at least 70 percent of the market. Both offer systems to cut fuel and electrical costs in large buildings. Devices that monitor and control air conditioning, lighting, and heating systems are tied together by information systems for managing the entire building. Since the early 70s, demand for this service has attracted other suppliers; so Honeywell and Johnson, to maintain their leading positions, have had to devise new strategies.

Honeywell's approach represents a strategic innovation thrust for reducing customer costs through the use of a new information processing capability.

For the manager of a building as small as 50,000 square feet who is neither willing nor able to acquire a computer, Honeywell offers DeltaNet, a service designed to eliminate the need for an on-site system.

Honeywell places sensors and controls in the building, ties them together in a local network, and transmits readings to 1 of 51

Honeywell processing centers in 26 cities. A center computer with a profile of the customer's building stored in its memory analyzes the transmitted data, determines what needs to be done, and sends commands back to the building automatically for action. This system, which took more than four years to develop, together with Honeywell's reputation for being a reliable supplier that provides installation and maintenance support, gives the firm a competitive edge in this newly formed segment. To enter it, the competition must match Honeywell's investment in time and information system resources.

Process innovations may occur at more than one point on a value-added chain. Benetton, Italy's largest sportswear manufacturer, exemplifies this kind of innovative multiplicity. Started in the 60s as a small factory operation by the Benetton family, the company has grown into a worldwide business with 2,600 franchised stores, nine plants, and sales of $351 million in 1983.

The key to Benetton's success, which some have called the "Italian miracle of the century," is its innovative application of computer technology at three points on its chain:

1.   Producing only for orders in hand, its inventory control system matches purchasing and production requirements. This cuts inventory-carrying costs and costs associated with demand misjudgments.

2.   Using its computer-aided design and manufacturing systems to lay out patterns and cut fabric waste to about 15 percent gives Benetton an advantage over rivals lacking such systems. Up to 40 percent of a manufacturer's cost goes to the purchase of raw materials such as fabric.

3.   Monitoring consumer preferences through on-line computer links to its principal agents and via point-of-sale terminals in its stores, Benetton predicts demand with a high degree of confidence. These monitoring systems allow it to respond ahead of the competition when changes in demand arise. The firm can, for example, dye goods to order and ship quickly so that within 10 days, sweaters, slacks, and the like are on the shelf of the store that placed the order.

Benetton's innovative thrusts at these points on its value-added chain set it apart from its rivals. Its strategic use of information systems is transforming the way business is conducted in the sportswear industry. With its systems expertise, it is in a position to respond rapidly to the fashions of the time.

CASE REFERENCES

American Hospital Supply   *Information Systems News*, August 9, 1982; *The Office*, December 1983; *The Wall Street Journal*, August 24, 1984; annual reports, 1981–83.

Batterymarch   *The Wall Street Journal*, May 8, 1984; November 9, 1984.

Benetton   *Business Week*, June 11, 1984.

Comp–U–Card   *Direct Marketing*, April 1981; *Computerworld*, January 23, 1984; *New York Times*, April 26, 1984.

Dallas Cowboys   *Business Week*, October 24, 1983; *Information Systems News*, November 16, 1981; *Popular Computing*, November 1982.

Dean Witter   *The Wall Street Journal*, November 15, 1982.

Democratic Party   *Information Systems News*, November 1, 1982; *New York Times*, September 22, 1983; January 28, 1984; February 15, 1984; April 23, 1984; *Business Week*, November 5, 1984.

Federal Express   *Inc.*, June 1984; *Computerworld*, August 8, 1983; annual reports, 1982–83.

First Boston   *Computer Decisions*, June 1984; *Computerworld*, September 5, 1983; *New York Times*, January 22, 1984; *The Wall Street Journal*, January 25, 1984.

Honeywell   *Business Week*, May 23, 1983; *The Wall Street Journal*, April 26, 1984.

Merrill Lynch   *New York Times*, November 21, 1982; November 20, 1983; *The Wall Street Journal*, November 15, 1982.

National Decision Systems   *New York Times*, August 21, 1983.

Phone In–Drive Thru   *Marketing News*, November 25, 1983.

Republican Party   See **Democratic Party.**

Reuters   *Business Week*, January 17, 1983; June 27, 1983; *Euromoney*, October 1983; *New York Times*, December 15, 1983; May 28, 1984; *The Wall Street Journal*, December 16, 1983; January 16, 1984; May 16, 1984.

BIBLIOGRAPHY

Hax, Arnoldo C., and Nicolas S. Majluf. *Strategic Management: An Integrative Perspective*. Englewood Cliffs, N.J.: Prentice-Hall, 1984.

Levitt, Theodore. *Marketing for Business Growth*. New York: McGraw-Hill, 1974.

MacMillan, Ian. "Preemptive Strategies." *Journal of Business Strategy*, Fall 1983.

Sutton, C. J. *Economics and Corporate Strategy*. Cambridge, England: Cambridge University Press, 1980.

Twiss, Brian. *Managing Technological Innovation*. 2d ed. London: Longman Group, 1980.

6

Growth

DIMENSIONS OF GROWTH

The growth of firms may be plotted along two dimensions: product and function. Product growth involves the firm's offerings—its various lines, sublines, and individual products. As such, it may entail the expansion of markets, satisfaction of additional customer needs, and adoption of alternative technologies associated with the product. Functional growth, on the other hand, involves the various functions (e.g., R&D, manufacturing, distribution, retailing) performed on the firm's product (industry, value-added) chain. Within this category, spinoffs constitute a special form of functional expansion.

The examples to follow illustrate the range of strategic growth opportunities open to firms with the vision to support or shape them through the use of information systems. Like its close relatives—differentiation, cost, and innovation—growth has bonds with other thrusts. A firm may execute a growth thrust, for example, that simultaneously reduces cost, differentiates its product, and innovates in the processing of customer orders.

GROWTH: PRODUCT

IBM offers a wide assortment of product lines to its customers: computers, peripherals, typewriters, supplies, telephone switches, and so on. Each line consists of groups of related products. In the computer line, for example, the mainframe group comprises 3033s, 3081s, and 4300s; the minicomputer group, 8100s and System/1s; the microcomputer group, PCs and PC Jrs.

For any product in an IBM line, three questions may be asked: (1) Who is it aimed at? (2) What needs does it satisfy? (3) How does it satisfy these needs? Answers to Question 1 determine the *customer groups* or *market segments* targeted. For consumer products, these may be specified by the values of a number of variables: geographic (region, country, city, climate), demographic (age, sex, family size/ life cycle, income, occupation, education, religion, race, nationality), psychographic (social class, lifestyle, personality), and behavioral (frequency of use, benefit sought, loyalty, readiness to buy, attitude toward product). For industrial products, markets may be segmented by industry, geography, size, etc.

Answers to Question 2 determine the *customer needs* met by the firm's product. An automatic teller machine, for example, may satisfy needs to receive cash, make deposits, and transfer funds from one account to another at any time.

Answers to Question 3 determine the *technologies* associated with the product. If the customer need is land transportation, alternative technologies include those associated with automobiles, trucks, tanks, bicycles, and so on. Answers to Question 3 also include the various channels through which the firm delivers its product to the customer.

The firm's products fall into various lines, depending on whether they satisfy sameness or similarity relations defined on customer groups, customer needs, technologies, distribution channels, prices, etc. The IBM PC and PC Jr. fall into the microcomputer line, being targeted at the same or similar customers, meeting roughly the same or similar needs, and selling through many of the same channels, within a price range that separates them from IBM's minicomputer line and from each other.

To *lengthen* its line, the firm can add new products. IBM entered the microcomputer market in 1981 with the PC. In 1983, it lengthened its microcomputer line by adding the PC Jr. model.

To *deepen* its line, the firm can add product variants. Building on the success of its PC, IBM deepened this line by introducing the PC/XT, a second version of the personal computer intended primarily for business use and distinguished from the firstborn by its extended data storage capacity.

To *widen* its line, the firm can add other lines, complementary or unrelated. Widening its PC computer line, IBM now offers a new line of color monitors, items previously unavailable from IBM (although sold by others) to purchasers of the PC.

Growth along the product dimension (i.e., *product growth*) may occur with respect to the addition of customer groups targeted, customer needs met, or technologies employed. It may result from the firm's decision to lengthen, deepen, or widen its lines. Such moves may be motivated by a desire to:

- Exploit underutilized resources, human or material, released in the course of the firm's normal business.
- Improve performance by reducing risk and uncertainty through product line diversification.
- Meet competitive thrusts posed by full-line rivals.
- Fill gaps between desired and projected sales.
- Prevent competitors, by denying them shelf space, from encroaching on the firm's territory.

The firm may also pursue a growth strategy along the product dimension by increasing the *intensity* of its involvement or penetration relative to customer groups, customer needs, or technologies. Here, no new groups are targeted, no new needs satisfied, and no new technologies introduced. What changes is the intensity of involvement or penetration. The firm may pursue a product growth strategy in a particular segment, for example, by hiring 25 more sales reps to sell its line.

Toys "Я" Us, the nationwide discount chain, opened 25 new toy stores in 1983, bringing its total to 169. By far the largest chain in the United States, Toys "Я" Us commanded an 11 percent share of the highly fragmented toy market. The company's winning game plan combines ample parking lots, good management, large, well-organized stores with thousands of items ranging from yo-yos to electronic games, and information systems. Among other things, the systems keep track of what's selling in all stores so that Toys can take quick markdowns to rid itself of slow movers. In the toy business, this application counts as an innovative strategic thrust transforming the traditional inventory control process.

But it also plays another strategic role for the company. Recently, Toys announced the formation of Kids "Я" Us, a new chain of children's apparel stores modeled after its toy supermarkets. This strategic move represents a product growth diversification thrust, widening the firm's existing line from toys to children's apparel. Just as information systems supported the company's strategy in the toy business, it can be expected to play a similar role in this new undertaking. More significant, however, is the fact that the system itself is being used to fuel the firm's diversification move, its expansion into a new industry.

Yet what led to advantage in one game might not apply in another. At least that's what the conventional wisdom on these matters holds. But Toy's move seems to have evoked considerable fear among at least 285 small specialty and department store owners across the United States. This may be inferred from the remarks of the president of a buying office in New York City that represents them. "This new chain has upset everyone in the market. You come up against a giant like this, with every major line discounted, and where do you go? If you're the average kiddy shop next door, do you take gas or cut your throat?"

On the other hand, being in a new league, Toys faces some formidable competition: Sears, J. C. Penney, and Federated Stores (a 102-store chain), to name a few. But this new competition shouldn't daunt Toys, which seems to be on a roll in the games it plays. At the close of 1984, it became the world's largest toy specialty retail chain operating about 200 toy stores in the United States, four in Canada, and one in Singapore. In addition, it ran four department stores and 10 children's clothing stores. Plans call for the opening of up to 45 new toy stores and 15 children's clothing stores in the United States, Canada, and Great Britain.

While Toys executed a strategic growth move by diversifying into a new industry, Wetterau, the fourth largest U.S. food wholesaler, followed a different recipe. Up to 1982, it prospered by concentrating on small, independent supermarkets. According to Ted Wetterau, the chairman, "the cornerstone of our whole business was that we would not service the chains."

But the slack economy in 1982 and a costly battle to defeat an unexpected takeover attempt in the fall of 1981 stalled the company's efforts to gain new business. Moreover, with the total number of independent grocers declining by 35 percent in 10 years (from 174,000 units in 1970 to 113,000 in 1980), Wetterau had to revise its strategy. For the first time, the St. Louis–based concern decided to offer its wide array of services and volume discounts to chains of 10 to 20 units, thus expanding its traditional customer groups.

Wetterau's know-how in computerized inventory control and electronic checkout (point of sale) systems backbones this product growth strategic thrust. With more than 100 scanner-equipped stores tied to its host computer, Wetterau updates prices, tracks re-ordering data, generates shelf labels, and performs other functions that supermarket executives hesitate to reveal, because a competitive edge may be lost. Can the technologically undernourished chains resist this appetizing bait? That's the question Wetterau seems to be betting its future on.

From St. Louis, we move now to Bentonville, a small town in the northwest corner of Arkansas, where Sam Walton plots the future of the company he founded over 22 years ago—Wal-Mart, the fastest growing retailer in the United States, with average annual sales growth of 39 percent between 1980 and 1984. Occupying key locations in rural communities of 5,000 to 15,000 people, spread over Arkansas, Missouri, Louisiana, Oklahoma, and Texas, Wal-Mart expects to continue its uninterrupted march across the United States. Current plans call for a doubling of sales every two or three years and geographical expansion of Alexandrian proportions— the opening of as many as 125 new stores annually. Second to K mart in the discount business, Wal-Mart (with sales of over $6 billion in 1984) is closing in on Woolworth and Montgomery Ward in the general retail marketplace.

As analyzed by Isadore Barmash, the *New York Times'* eminent retailing specialist, Wal-Mart's past conquests and future prospects combine "an aggressive expansion with a state-of-the-art computerized merchandise information system, a strong distribution network, and a progressive employee relations program." By offering low prices and name brands, the chain dominates the market wherever it has stores. Using the information generated by its system strategically, Wal-Mart pressures suppliers to lower their prices and thereby help it operate as a low-cost discounter.

Like Kids "Я" Us and Wetterau, Wal-Mart successfully pursues a product growth strategic thrust backed by information systems that deliver. Computer technology at Kids supported a diversification move into another industry, at Wetterau a thrust into a new market segment, and at Wal-Mart a territorial expansion drive.

Similar stories can be told in other industries, as can be seen from the recent strategic growth thrusts executed by *The Wall Street Journal* and Yellow Freight Systems.

On January 31, 1984, Dow Jones & Company approved a $155 million plan to expand plant and press capacity for *The Wall Street Journal*. In 1982–83, Dow Jones authorized $55 million for similar expansion. According to the *Journal*, "the expansion will accommodate circulation increases and meet news and advertising space needs in the latter part of this decade." The chairman of Dow Jones reported that most of its publications and services operated at record levels in 1983, with advertising at the *Journal* increasing by 8.2 percent and circulation by more than 60,000 to over 2.1 million.

The *Journal's* product growth strategy depends on satellite technology and information systems associated with it. Dow Jones pioneered in this area, being the first private company in the United States licensed to own and operate its own earth stations. These stations transmit full pages of the *Journal* from five originating plants to a satellite that beams them to a dozen *Journal* printing facilities across the United States. In Hong Kong, the Asian edition, employing the same satellite know-how, sends its pages to a *Journal* printing plant in Singapore.

To talk of growth in the trucking industry, with its landscape littered with the wrecks of the worst shakeout since the depression in the 30s, one might be accused of gross insensitivity or worse. Yet deregulation here, as it has in the airline and financial service sectors, produces winners as well as losers. Among the former is Yellow Freight, the nation's third largest trucking company, based in Shawnee Mission, Kansas.

During the recession of the early 80s, Yellow's management expanded its operations in the less-than-full truckload business. It supported this product growth strategic thrust by investing heavily in the construction of new terminals, increasing its network from 248 in 1980 to 440 in 1983. But Yellow's expansion required more than terminals. It demanded investments in information and tele-communication systems as well. To track partial shipments across the country, to grow from $776.4 million to an expected $1.05 billion in 1983 would have been impossible without an elaborate electronic network.

Lengthening the product line represents a different form of product growth. For a manufacturer, this almost invariably translates into adding another kind of physical object to be sold. Service organizations, on the other hand, tend to supplement their offerings by hiring those with the requisite new service skills, assuming current staff members are fully occupied. Alternatively, technology can be used to shape the growth thrust.

DePaola, Begg & Associates, a small Hyannis, Massachusetts, CPA office followed this latter path. With 75 accounts in the mid-70s, the 15-year-old firm was eager to expand its services. The president, Tom DePaola, saw an opportunity to provide *on-line* general ledger, accounts receivable, payroll, and accounts payable processing for his clients. After installing a minicomputer, purchasing some standard programs, and developing a few of its own, De-Paola, Begg expanded its client base within 2½ years to 350, increasing revenues by 50 percent and staff by only three.

Another New England service organization, Inncorp, a manager of hotels and conference centers in the region, supported its product growth thrust in a somewhat different fashion. As the owner and operator of five hotels employing over 1,000 people, its five-year plan called for the acquisition of six more units by the end of the period.

To achieve its growth objectives and maintain profitability, Inncorp moved, through the strategic use of information systems, to centralize and integrate its activities. Prior to its growth thrust, the company permitted each hotel to operate independently, with its own accounting staff, purchasing department and so on. With the acquisition of a computer and the development of software, Inncorp reduced the number of local staff required to run a hotel, negotiated volume purchasing agreements to cover all its units, and cut its general operating expenses.

GROWTH: FUNCTION

Firms proffer many reasons for increasing their participation at critical points along the industry chain: lower cost, greater control, competitive pressure, and so on. But for our purposes here, the *direction* of functional growth interests us more than the *motive* for it.

The firm can grow via *backward expansion* if it involves itself in the functions performed by any of its generic suppliers, from raw material vendors to those who provide services. Involvement is *complete* if the firm acquires a supplier; otherwise, *partial*. Partial involvement takes different forms, from performing some or all of the functions normally undertaken by a supplier to acquiring some but not all of the supplier's equity. IBM followed a partial backward growth thrust when it acquired a 15 percent share of the Rolm Corp., a leading manufacturer of telephone switching systems (devices considered by many to be essential ingredients in the office automation marketplace), for $228 million. Subsequently, IBM decided on complete involvement and acquired Rolm. Earlier, IBM bought a 12 percent stake in Intel Corporation, a leading manufacturer of semiconductors and IBM's source for the chips powering its PC.

A firm can grow via *forward expansion* if it involves itself in the functions performed by any of its generic customers, from intermediaries to those selling its products to end users. Involvement here, as with backward expansion, can be complete or partial. IBM followed a partial forward expansion thrust when it opened its own computer stores to perform the functions of retailers, like Computerland and Sears, Roebuck & Company, that market many of the products sold in IBM outlets.

In the service sphere, computer-backed functional growth thrusts pose threats to the revenue streams of telephone, health insurance, and pension management organizations. These and other service businesses have recently been brought under complete or partial corporate control through the use of information systems.

"We want to control our own destiny." This sentence, usually uttered vehemently by leaders of newly independent states, comes now from the mouth of a Citicorp vice president. He used it in offering a rationale for his firm's backward expansion move into voice and data transmission services. "We got rid of Ma Bell years ago," he continued, "long before it became fashionable. Within New York, we have our own telephone network, with our own fiber-optic links and switches." Nationally, Citicorp *owns* its own satellite network, Citisatcom, having purchased transponders on Western Union's Westar 5 satellite. With earth stations in San Mateo, Los Angeles, San Francisco, Sioux Falls, and New York connected to Westar (and others planned for the near future), Citicorp's dream of telecommunication independence has become at least a partial reality.

In the United States, for example, it uses Citisatcom to operate regional credit and collection centers. These handle its more than 5 million Visa and MasterCard accounts, 80 percent of them outside New York State. In the emerging world of electronic banking, at least as Citicorp envisions it, a versatile and powerful telecommunications network is a necessary condition for success. When Citibank markets "electronic banking," it means

> handling the request, production, and delivery of our services. We offer customers the ability to electronically obtain and control the specific Citibank services they need whenever and wherever they need them. Our primary electronic banking goal is to deliver *all* our services electronically, and secondly, over time, also integrate our services, delivery mechanisms, and access technologies.[18]

Internally, the net provides bulk data and voice communication, interactive computing, database access, facsimile transmission, and videoconferencing.

While opportunities to reduce and avoid cost certainly encouraged Citicorp's move, its strategic vision demanded it. Citicorp sees itself as a global provider of a full line of financial services to businesses and individuals. According to its vice president for communications, "We had to ensure that we have the telecommunications capacity to meet our needs. . . . In some cases, the capabilities we need are just not available today from common carriers." To pursue its pioneering path in the new world of deregulated financial services, Citicorp internalized telecommunication services, making them an integral part of its competitive strategy.

While perhaps not integral to strategy in most organizations, telecommunication is hardly a trivial matter, constituting as it does the third largest administrative expense after payroll and property outlays. With a private network, a firm can at least control the cost of services among its own facilities. According to a recent estimate, a firm can obtain a 30–70 percent return on investment (ROI) within an 18-month payback period. Atlantic Richfield, for example, operates ARCOnet, a $20 million top-of-the-line system providing voice, data, and teleconferencing services. Electronic traffic flows through satellite pipelines linking Alaska's north slope to ARCO headquarters in Los Angeles, to its data center in Dallas, and to other locations across the country.

The Harris Corporation, a large electronics firm located in Florida, erected a satellite net to link its various plants in Texas, California, and Rhode Island. According to company officials, the net saves Harris over $1 million a year and develops valuable know-how for use elsewhere.

Backward expansion made possible by information systems proceeds in other service areas as well. In Lincolnton, North Carolina, Cochrane Furniture now processes about 400 health insurance claims each month for its approximately 725 employees and their families. Cochrane had been paying $40 thousand a year in administrative service charges to a major insurance company. Instead of developing its own system to do the processing, Cochrane bought a turnkey system which required no additional staff to operate; personnel formerly handling health benefits were trained to run it.

In the pension management field, the integration theme repeats itself. Air Canada's managers now run a $1.25 billion fund, where formerly this work was subcontracted to bank and trust companies, the organizations actually holding the securities. These financial institutions reported on the maturity dates of securities, transactions, and cash on hand. In general, however, they didn't provide daily data on current assets or earned income; nor did they develop cash forecasts.

With its new pension management system, Air Canada no longer needs nor pays for these outside services. But compared to the benefits of more timely, critical investment information, this is small change. The new in-house application tracks settlement deadlines and alerts managers when payments on account are due, payments that in the past were often delayed by security brokers, banks, or trust companies. "A difference of one or two days in settlements can mean a loss of hundreds of thousands annually for a fund as large as ours," said the carrier's senior vice president for corporate finance and planning.

GROWTH: SIS SPINOFFS

The firm can grow via *projective expansion*, or *vertical disintegration* as some have dubbed it, if it projects resources dedicated to a functional activity into a new, independent business unit dedicated to selling the goods or services associated with the function. In such cases, the line between product and functional growth vanishes. A manufacturer with a large fleet of trucks engaged in transporting its products may decide to create a new business unit to provide freight-hauling services for shippers located along its principal routes. Similarly, a firm may create a business unit with resources drawn from its information management function. I call such strategic growth thrusts *strategic information systems spinoffs*.

The recent move by Intermountain Health Care, a holding company with a nonprofit subsidiary and a growing list of profit-oriented units, illustrates the SIS spinoff idea. Faced with rising costs, patient declines, and competition from profit-making hospitals and newly formed groups of specialized physicians, the Intermountain chain of 23 hospitals in Utah, Wyoming, and Idaho reorganized in 1982 to form IHC. The chain itself became the nonprofit subsidiary.

Among the units dedicated to profit, IHC created an SIS spinoff, a purchasing arm that buys over $500 million worth of supplies and equipment for 125 other hospitals, an operation to provide hospitals with insurance, and a variety of specialized clinics and occupational health care centers. Shortly after its launch, the spinoff signed contracts for processing services, with 24 of the 125 hospitals already benefiting from IHS's volume purchase deals. The five-year plan calls for an expansion of data processing services to at least 100 hospitals.

While the SIS spinoff just described is still in its infancy, others (like those spawned by McDonnell Douglas, the aerospace company, and General Electric) have been growing for over two decades. In the early 60s, McDonnell created McAuto (McDonnell Douglas Automation Company) and GE formed Geisco (General Electric Information Services Company) to leverage their internal investments in computer technology. The paths pursued by these two companies should be of interest to those with infants or with thoughts of SIS spinoff thrusts.

McDonnell originally chartered McAuto to provide consulting, systems analysis and design, programming, and remote processing services for its divisions and for anyone else willing to pay. GE established Geisco to exploit the concept of time-sharing, which it had developed internally. In 1970, 85 percent of Geisco's revenue came from this segment of its business; a similar percentage of McAuto's revenues were derived at the time from its processing operations.

Since 1970, however, both organizations have diversified to reduce their dependence on the increasingly competitive commodity-like processing business. Today, the magic word is *value-added*.

Consider, for example, McAuto's position in the health care industry. In the early 70s, it acquired a group dedicated to providing data processing services and applications to hospitals. From a customer base of 21 at its inception, McAuto's Health Services Division has now installed systems in over 1,500 hospitals across the country.

In 1979, McAuto acquired Microdata, a manufacturer of minicomputer systems. This led to the development of a new product line, turnkey systems for hospitals that run on Microdata computers and use software (for patient registration, control, and accounting and for payroll, general ledger, accounts payable, and other conventional applications) created by analysts and programmers from the Health Services Division.

During the 70s, through internal development and alliances, McAuto expanded its offerings to include on-line financial control systems for hospitals and systems for nurses, physicians, and clinical laboratories. Indeed, the Health Services Division presents itself to hospitals as "the single source for all your data processing needs."

In the early 80s, after determining that its aerospace operations would probably level off in the 90s, McDonnell formulated a new growth strategy. It decided to become a major player in the fast-growing information services industry. Using its successful experience in health care as a model, McDonnell created a major new division, the Information Services Group (ISG), which it organized by industry. The health services unit, for example, comprises the Health Services Division of McAuto, portions of Microdata, and Vitek, a manufacturer of automated laboratory testing equipment acquired by McAuto in the 70s. Other units target the telecommunication, manufacturing, financial service, and travel industries.

To implement this new SIS vision, ISG made the following thrusts:

1. Acquisition of Tymshare, an information services company that operates Tymnet, the largest nationwide, public, value-added data communications network. Tymnet provides a mechanism for users of incompatible devices, such as terminals and computers, to communicate with each other. "We're going to sell Tymnet as a public network that anybody can use—and develop businesses around it," says an ISG official. As the initial venture, the health services unit expects to build a nationwide health claims clearinghouse for insurance companies that will make use of the net. In the electronic funds transfer sector, Tymshare plays an important role as the largest credit card processor in the world and, through its acquisition of Telecheck, as a provider of point-of-sale services to merchants (e.g., check guarantees, credit verification).

2. Acquisition of Computer Sharing Services, a supplier of computer services to Bell operating companies, AT&T, and others. CSS fits into ISG's new $100 million telecommunications unit.

3. Agreement with IBM to sell CAD/CAM software developed by ISG's manufacturing unit that will run on IBM minicomputers. Estimates put the cost of a typical system, consisting of an IBM minicomputer, software, and four workstations, at about $600,000.

4. Acquisition of Science Dynamics Corp., a supplier of information systems for physicians. SDC fits into ISG's health services unit.

With its evolving SIS vision of industry-by-industry penetration, McDonnell's SIS spinoff shapes its destiny through the execution of strategic thrusts like the ones just mentioned. How effective these thrusts will be depends on a number of factors not the least of which are the strategies and moves of ISG's rivals. Among them, ISG counts GE. "They've said point-blank that they want to be in the factory of the future," a top ISG executive said. "So they're going to be competing with us." But if its strategic intelligence system identifies just GE's factory automation efforts as threatening, ISG is in for a surprise. For the SIS vision of GE's Geisco calls for thrusts in many of the industries staked by ISG as areas of opportunity.

Consider, for example, Geisco's Easy-Claim system, a computerized claims-processing and office automation package for physicians. First installed at Blue Shield of Illinois, it allows physicians to file claims automatically through a computer in their offices, eliminating errors and payment delays. This innovative application signals Geisco's intention of developing a position in the health care industry.

Behind it lies one of the most powerful and extensive infrastructures in the information services industry, comprising such facilities as:

- Mark III, the world's largest commercial teleprocessing network. Customers may connect to the net by placing a local telephone call in more than 750 cities, in 24 countries, in 23 time zones, 24 hours a day, 365 days a year; worldwide, Geisco counts over 6,000 users of Mark III.

- MarkNet, a value-added network like ISG's Tymnet or GTE's Telenet, which reaches over 600 cities in the United States. Designed to handle data, text, and graphics, with plans to support image and voice processing, MarkNet allows users of terminals from over 36 vendors to communicate with personal computers from IBM, Wang, Apple, Tandy, and others.
- Quick-Comm, an electronic mail system, which is part of Geisco's plan for providing end-to-end document distribution services.
- A range of software packages and systems.
- A worldwide staff of consultants, system designers, and the like to support Geisco's products.

Today, less than 30 percent of Geisco's revenues come from its processing operations; this percentage is expected to shrink to about 10 percent as it expands its line with more proprietary products. Being part of GE, a corporation that takes pride in its ability to manage strategically, Geisco finds itself encouraged to transform its identity from a commodity operation to a full-service, value-added colossus.

For GE sees itself as "in the business of creating businesses," businesses expected to be number one or two in their industries. At the GE board of directors meeting in April 1981, Jack Welch, GE's new chairman and CEO, expressed his strategic vision as follows:

> A decade from now we would like General Electric to be perceived as a unique, high spirited, entrepreneurial enterprise . . . a company known around the world for its unmatched level of excellence. We want GE to be the most profitable highly diversified company on earth, with world quality leadership in every one of its product lines.

Welch's tone and imprint are already having their effect. As one GE executive put it, "He wants GE to make money, to develop an 'unfair advantage' over the competition, to reflect top quality, and to put bright people in to run the businesses."[19]

In August 1981, Welch announced the formation of three sectors to manage GE's multiplicity of businesses, ranging from aircraft engines to light bulbs. Two of GE's fastest growing businesses found their new home in the services and materials sector: the General Electric Credit Corp. (GECC) and Geisco. The strategic slogan for this sector is "growth and integration," which means (among other things) closer ties between GECC and Geisco. In 1983, GE made acquisitions and other investments totaling about $650 million in this sector.

Supported by GE's new strategic imperatives, Geisco's management formulated programs to implement its SIS vision. According to Geisco's senior vice president for programs and management operations:

> The only way we're going to get big in packaged software is through acquisition. We want to keep growing in that area. . . . My long-term competition is AT&T and IBM. Those are the people I worry about and the people I think about when I'm deciding what strategy to use and what kind of capabilities we need. . . . We've seen IBM move into insurance. . . . They've built a position in insurance. . . . Maybe we've done the same in banking, and AT&T will pull it off in something else. Have I targeted the industries where we should be going? Yes, but I'd rather not say what they are. That would give those two more information than I want to give them.[20]

To enhance its position in the packaged software and microcomputer distribution markets, Geisco executed the following thrusts:

- Acquisition of Software International, a leading producer of accounting, financial, and manufacturing software.
- Acquisition of Energy Enterprises, a software house specializing in on-line monitoring and evaluation systems for over 250 gas and oil industry customers.
- Acquisition of Banking Systems, a software company supplying banks with automatic teller, bill payment, and data entry systems.

- Acquisition of LTI (formerly Lambda) Consulting, a software consulting firm focusing on large mainframe and minicomputer systems.
- Agreements with IBM and Apple to resell PCs and Macintoshes with value-added Geisco software and optional installation and maintenance services.

These thrusts signal Geisco's intention of establishing information systems positions in the manufacturing, energy, and banking industries. If McDonnell's ISG group failed to identify this giant as a rival in the past, it has ample evidence to draw the inference now.

The evolution of McAuto and Geisco, the 60s' spinoffs of McDonnell and GE, reflect increasingly complex SIS visions. In both cases, further growth will depend, even more than it has in the past, on their ability to forge SIS alliances, the subject we turn to next.

CASE REFERENCES

Air Canada   *Computerworld*, November 28, 1983.

Apple Computer   See GE (Geisco).

ARCO   *Information Systems News*, October 31, 1983: *The Office*, November 1983.

Banking Systems   See GE (Geisco).

Citibank   *Business Week*, September 5, 1983; *Communications Week*, August 13, 1984; *Electronic Banking: An Executive's Guide* (Citibank); *Information Systems News*, October 31, 1983; *The Wall Street Journal*, March 29, 1984.

Cochrane Furniture   *Computerworld*, November 14, 1983.

Computer Sharing Services   See McDonnell Douglas (McAuto).

DePaola, Begg & Associates   *InfoSystems*, September 1981.

Energy Enterprises   See GE (Geisco).

GE (Geisco)   *Computerworld*, September 12, 1983; *Datamation*, February 1983; *Information Systems News*, April 16, 1984; *The Wall Street Journal*, December 14, 1984; "GE Strategic Position 1981," Harvard Business School Case Studies: 1981; "GE—Business Development," Harvard Business School Case Studies: 1982; Annual Report, 1983.

Harris   *The Office*, November 1982.

Inncorp   *Computerworld*, November 30, 1981.

Intermountain Health Care   *Business Week*, May 16, 1983.

Kids "Я" Us   *The New York Times*, December 28, 1984; *The Wall Street Journal*, August 25, 1983; November 23, 1983.

LTI   See GE (Geisco).

McDonnell Douglas (McAuto)   *Management Technology,* September 1984; *The Wall Street Journal,* March 7, 1984; March 13, 1984; March 20, 1984; November 16, 1984; December 6, 1984; Ulric Weil, *Information Systems in the 80s: Products, Markets, and Vendors* (Englewood Cliffs, N.J.: Prentice-Hall, 1982).

Microdata   See McDonnell Douglas (McAuto).

Science Dynamics Corp.   See McDonnell Douglas (McAuto).

Software International   See GE (Geisco).

Telecheck   See McDonnell Douglas (McAuto).

Toys "Я" Us   See Kids "Я" Us.

Tymshare   See McDonnell Douglas (McAuto).

Vitek   See McDonnell Douglas (McAuto).

The Wall Street Journal   *The Wall Street Journal,* January 24, 1983, advertisement; January 31, 1984.

Wal-Mart   *The New York Times,* July 1, 1984; *The Wall Street Journal,* July 2, 1984.

Wetterau   *Business Week,* February 22, 1982.

Yellow Freight   *The New York Times,* December 13, 1983.

BIBLIOGRAPHY

Abell, Derek. *Defining the Business*. Englewood Cliffs, N.J.: Prentice-Hall, 1980.

Kotler, Philip. *Marketing Management: Analysis, Planning, and Control*. 5th ed. Englewood Cliffs, N.J.: Prentice-Hall, 1984.

Robinson, E. A. G. *The Structure of Competitive Industry*. 2d ed. Chicago: University of Chicago, 1958.

Thomas, R. E. *Business Policy*. 2d ed. Oxford: Philip Allen, 1983.

7

SIS Alliances

ALLIANCES

As I use the term, *alliance* means any combination of two or more groups or individuals joined together for the purpose of achieving a common objective. By this definition, mergers are alliances. Some might find this unacceptable, arguing that combinations failing to preserve the separate identities of the partners should not be counted as alliances. Granted, a case could be made for narrowing the sense of the term in this fashion. But for our purposes, it pays to adopt a more catholic position, admitting mergers and acquisitions (whether partial or complete), as legitimate alliance forms. This broader conception opens, as we shall soon see, a rich vein of strategic initiative opportunities in which information systems play a critical part.

Strategic alliances are intra- or interfirm combinations designed to support or shape the competitive strategy of one or more of the allies. Such alliances take a variety of forms. For example, Japan's Suzuki Motor Company manufactures Chevrolet's Sprint minicars and ships them to GM dealers; GM owns 34.2 percent of Suzuki. GM and Toyota, the world's two largest automobile companies, together roll Chevrolet Nova subcompacts off the line at their Freemont, California, plant. Partial acquisition (GM/Suzuki) and a 50–50 joint venture (GM/Toyota) represent two forms of strategic alliance. With both GM/Suzuki and GM/Toyota, GM hopes to exploit the automotive production capabilities of these Japanese firms and thereby support its worldwide cost reduction strategy.

There are three generic strategic alliance forms: acquisition, joint venture, and agreement. To count as a *strategic acquisition alliance* in which X acquires (partially or completely) Y, the alliance X/Y must be such that Y performs some function on X's product chain or produces a product related to X's product line. With these stipulations, I exclude those mergers and acquisitions often dubbed "unrelated." For it hardly makes sense to talk of the competitive strategy of a conglomerate with unrelated business units or divisions in its portfolio.

In a *strategic joint venture alliance*, X and Y may participate in varying degrees, from a 50–50 partnership like the GM/Toyota deal to myriad other proportional arrangements. Unpopular for many years in the United States, joint ventures are now undergoing a government-sponsored renaissance.

In the mid-80s at least, the Justice Department no longer looks suspiciously at these combinations. Indeed, the department's attitude now seems to encourage them. In 1984, the head of its Antitrust Division indicated the agency would not oppose ventures, even between rivals in concentrated markets, if efficiencies could be expected as a result of the deal. He told the New England Antitrust Conference that "an awareness of the role these valuable business arrangements play in creating efficiencies and bringing forth new products and technologies is replacing an attitude of suspicion born of ignorance." Further, he claimed that joint ventures "will play a vital role in promoting the growth and international competitiveness of the American economy."

Under a *strategic agreement alliance*, X and Y negotiate an agreement whereby X licenses Y to use its product or process, or X produces a product and Y uses, distributes, markets, or otherwise augments it to form some new offering that Y sells. In each of the strategic alliance forms just sketched (acquisition, joint venture, and agreement), the defining conditions can be extended easily to cases involving more than two organizations.

When X and Y forge an alliance, X may exploit the resources of Y that it lacks, Y might exploit the resources of X that it lacks, or both may exploit the resources of another party in addition to their own. In GM/Suzuki, GM exploits the production capabilities of Suzuki, and Suzuki exploits GM's dealer network.

The source of the resource to be exploited depends on your point of view. When brainstorming for alliance opportunities, three questions related to the required resource should be addressed:

1. Do we possess it?
2. Does another organization possess it?
3. Does it need to be created?

In other words, is the key resource yours, theirs, or other—something that must be created by you, your ally, both of you working together, or by another party?

Combining alliance forms with resource sources opens up nine possible strategic alliance moves (see Figure 7-1). If we possess the key resource (Opportunities 1-3), can we find an ally via acquisition, joint venture, or agreement that possesses resources we need to exploit the key resource?

If we lack the key resource (Opportunities 4-6), do we possess resources that we could exploit by forging an alliance via acquisition, joint venture, or agreement with an organization possessing the key resource?

Finally, if we lack the key resource because it doesn't exist but we possess another exploitable resource, can we find an ally via acquisition, joint venture, or agreement that will develop the key resource or, using its resources and ours, find another organization that can create the key resource (Opportunities 7-9)?

If your organization has developed information systems assets, then the examples cited below should stimulate your thoughts on how to identify and design strategic initiatives that will leverage these resources. But if your cache of information system assets to

Figure 7-1   SIS alliance opportunities

Form of Alliance

Source of Resource		Acquisition	Joint venture	Agreement
	Yours	1	2	3
	Theirs	4	5	6
	Other	7	8	9

parlay is skimpy, don't lose hope. You may be able to exploit the information systems developed by others.

Such considerations lead naturally to the question: Why do firms make alliances? As the reader may have surmised, the motives for strategic alliances are found among the strategic thrusts of differentiation, cost, innovation, and growth. Alliances are forged to enable the organization to:

Further differentiate its product.

Reduce the differentiation advantages of its strategic targets.

Reduce its costs.

Raise the costs of its competitors.

Develop innovative products or processes.

Imitate those who have developed such products or processes.

Grow by expanding customer groups, customer needs satisfied, technologies used, or functions controlled.

All of these, and others, serve as ground(s) for alliance formation.

Being tied so intimately to such moves, should strategic alliances be considered as independent thrusts—different in kind, not just in form, from the others? On theoretical grounds, perhaps not. But practically, there are two reasons for treating them separately as thrusts in their own right. First, they are commonly understood in the popular press, as strategic moves. Second, there may be other objectives served by such alliances, purposes not met by the strategic thrusts of differentiation, cost, innovation, and growth.

Information systems may be used to support or shape strategic alliance thrusts. I call such thrusts, not unexpectedly, *SIS (strategic information system) alliances*. The class of strategic information system alliances that can be used in conjunction with the firm's other strategic thrusts may take the form of an acquisition, joint venture, or agreement and may exploit your key information system assets, those of your ally, or those that will be developed as a result of the alliance. The examples below illustrate the range of opportunities open to firms with the vision to use information systems assets to gain competitive advantage through the use of strategic alliances.

I have classified these opportunities into four groups: product integration, product distribution, product extension, and product development. Each case, however, may also be seen from the vantage point of the thrust it exemplifies. The fourfold scheme introduced here encourages, I believe, the identification of SIS alliance opportunities.

ALLIANCES: PRODUCT INTEGRATION

Product integration alliances create new offerings by bringing together parts or all of products that can be sold separately. The amount of value added in this process shows great variation. In some cases, the offering merely places in one box what normally would be packaged in two. In others, it weaves the products of the partners into an organic whole whose parts are inseparable.

The cases to follow illustrate this variety. I have divided them into four classes, depending on the number and kind of ingredients involved. In *simple turnkey alliances*, the offering comprises a single information system and a single hardware system on which it runs; in *complex turnkey alliances*, more than one information or hardware system is involved. In *simple software alliances*, the offering comprises the combination of two information systems or modules of information systems. In *complex software alliances*, more than two systems or modules are involved. In general, product integration alliances enable some partners to expand their product lines.

Simple Turnkey Alliances

Computervision Corp., the revenue leader in CAD/CAM software, formed a simple turnkey alliance with IBM whereby it became a value-added remarketer of certain IBM computer models. While it is Computervision's closest competitor in this marketplace, IBM realizes that it cannot satisfy the needs of customers in every niche. Most analysts believe that the agreement will increase the sales of both vendors.

Comshare, Inc., a leading time-sharing company and developer of a decision support system software tool called System W, also signed a complementary marketing agreement with IBM. Under the terms of this pact, IBM markets System W through its sales force, while Comshare provides leads to IBM for its 4300 series of computers and retains the rights to the package. IBM sells 4300s and Comshare sells System Ws. The IBM connection should enable Comshare to develop a good position with users of 4300s. As a result of this simple turnkey SIS alliance, Comshare gains significant competitive advantage over its numerous rivals. It is now counted as one of the leading decision support package vendors, having been a minor player prior to its agreement with IBM. The pact also helps the company diversify from time-sharing, its principal but declining line of business, into the fast-growing sphere of packaged software.

Geisco, General Electric's information services company (also in the time-sharing business) forged a simple turnkey agreement with IBM in which it became a value-added remarketer of the IBM PC. Geisco sees this as an SIS alliance opportunity to leverage some of the information systems it offers on its network by repackaging/modifying them for the PC.

IBM has signed similar pacts with firms possessing valuable data bases and related information systems. Mead Data's complementary marketing agreement with IBM permits users to access the firm's Lexis and Nexis data bases via the IBM PC, the Displaywriter, and other IBM terminal devices. Originally, Mead made Lexis and Nexis available only to those who had leased Mead's terminal.

Complex Turnkey Alliances

The John Hancock Mutual Life Insurance Company solved the problem of providing its agents with computing power by forming a complex turnkey alliance. Unlike Fireman's Fund (see below), which acquired a software producer to attend to its agents' needs,

John Hancock assembled an offering composed of such items as a PC from IBM, a spreadsheet from Lotus, a word-processing package from Softword, and a system for developing policy proposals from its own (in-house) microcomputer programming staff. When an agent orders the turnkey system, John Hancock's data processing department handles the entire transaction, from putting the pieces together to delivery, training, and so on.

Blue Cross and Blue Shield (BC/BS) of Greater New York, which serves over 25,000 physicians in a 17-county region, offers a complex turnkey system to speed the submission of claims from doctors and perform a variety of office functions. The system, Amicus I, cuts six or more days off reimbursement time, produces reminder letters for delinquent accounts, lists patients according to diagnostic category, and "streamlines office operations, communications, and financial transactions among physicians, patients, and private and public health insurers."

BC/BS developed this system by forming alliances with IBM (IBM PC), Okidata (Microline 93 printer), Hayes Microcomputer Products (Smartmodem 1200), and Davong Systems (tape backup unit). Along with software, installation, and support, BC/BS offers Amicus I for $16,200 to the estimated 85 percent of physicians in the area lacking computer support.

Simple Software Alliances

Applied Data Research, a leading developer of database, data communications and other system software packages, recently inked agreements with two archrivals in the application software business, Management Science America and McCormack & Dodge, the Dun & Bradstreet subsidiary. These pacts are defensive alliances struck in response to Cullinet Software's full-line strategy of offering integral system and application packages. Under the terms of these alliances, the partners will cooperate in both developing and marketing their integrated wares.

Along somewhat similar lines, Software AG, another system software house, has signed at least 10 joint marketing agreements with application development firms. Software AG offers its "software engine," consisting of modules from its database management system (Adabas) and its fourth-generation query language (Natural), to replace whatever routines the applications use to handle data management and retrieval functions. Here, the application vendor gets the added value of a popular database system, and the system's house penetrates accounts it might not otherwise reach.

Information Sciences, a software vendor specializing in human resources and payroll applications, made a different kind of arrangement with Artificial Intelligence, Inc. when it signed a marketing pact with them. AI, the developer of an easy-to-use query package called "Intellect," provides copies of its code to InfoSci's customers. This gives them access to personnel and payroll data bases when unexpected calls for information arise.

Do simple software alliances lead inevitably to a pot of gold? Management Science America (MSA) (a large mainframe software producer), evidently believed that they did when it purchased Peachtree, a leading microcomputer software house. Unfortunately for MSA, however, its alliance with Peachtree foundered. "We diversified into something that we aren't expert in," lamented MSA's chairman in December 1984, when announcing that Peachtree was for sale. But he maintained that the alliance, while a financial disaster, has some benefits: MSA acquired Peachtree in 1981 in part to learn how mainframe and microcomputer might be linked. In this regard at least, according to its head, MSA gained valuable know-how.

Complex Software Alliances

Extendicare Ltd., a Toronto conglomerate that owns Crown Life Insurance Company (one of Canada's largest) and Crowntek (a recently formed, high-technology subsidiary), acquired the Computer Corporation of America (CCA), a Cambridge-based software house. CCA will be folded into Crowntek, becoming part of a group that includes Kaptron (a developer of fiber-optic communications devices), Polaris Technology (a software and consulting company that is the Canadian distributor of CCA's product line), and Waterloo Micro Systems (a microcomputer software developer).

Extendicare believes the acquisition of CCA will yield synergistic products, due to the close bonds expected to form among Crowntek's stable of entrepreneurs. Just six months after its announcement, the first fruits of this alliance ripened. CCA announced an office automation product that includes a microcomputer operating system developed by Waterloo and a file transfer package from Polaris.

The recently created Inter-Financial Software joint venture represents another kind of complex software alliance. In this situation, three software companies, Hogan Systems, Monchik-Weber, and Continuum, decided to work together on satisfying the converging needs of their customers for new information systems-based products and services. Currently, each firm provides systems and services to segments of the financial market. Hogan's customers are commercial banks; Monchik-Weber's clients are securities and investment management firms; Continuum provides systems to individual life, health, and annuity companies in the insurance industry. The new organization, Inter-Financial, will produce *integrated* information systems for customers who need systems that cut across the banking, brokerage, and insurance fields.

ALLIANCES: PRODUCT DISTRIBUTION

Product distribution alliances create new channels of distribution for a product. In the cases to follow, either the product itself or the channel of distribution is based on information systems.

American Express's acquisition of Investors Diversified Services (IDS) from the Alleghany Corporation reflects this kind of SIS alliance. While legally unlike the Israeli-Jamaican partnership described below, the $773 million deal between American Express and Alleghany is similar in objective: to leverage existing information system assets.

American Express saw in IDS a vehicle for distributing, either electronically or through the IDS sales force, the myriad of its information systems–based financial products and services, including those developed by its various units: Shearson in the brokerage area, Fireman's Fund in the insurance realm, etc. The acquisition permits the financial giant to tap into IDS's massive market of over 1.1 million customers, located primarily in small and medium-sized cities. Previously, American Express's only penetration point had been through the direct mail route. Now it uses IDS's 4,500 salespeople who already peddle mutual funds, tax shelters, and other investment to their clients.

Electronic Data Systems (EDS), the large Dallas-based information system company recently acquired by General Motors, provides facilities management and remote data processing services nationwide. Under alliances forged with Hogan Systems and Cullinet Software, EDS enlarged the range of systems it offers to customers and enabled these software companies to penetrate market segments previously inaccessible to them.

Hogan and Cullinet sell expensive systems that only the largest organizations can afford to purchase. By making their wares available to EDS customers via the latter's regional processing centers, both vendors hope to gain access to new groups of users from smaller firms. In the case of Hogan, for example, its software—originally designed for banks with more than $1 billion in assets—is now available to over 700 EDS banking customers, the majority with under $1 billion in assets. According to Hogan's president, "this agreement opens up a new market for our software. With EDS, our software will now serve institutions of all sizes." By making its powerful database management system available to small users via the EDS network, Cullinet also expands its customer base.

SIS alliances can be arranged with competitors as well as with suppliers and customers. In the demilitarized zone of financial services, rivals or potential rivals (one is never quite sure here) often find it profitable to trade with each other. This is particularly true when your potential partner is a player in a financial services sector encroaching on your territory. For example, Dreyfus Corp., the large mutual fund outfit, recently made a deal with Chase Manhattan Bank to manage funds for its clients. Bank of America has arranged with a large insurance company to provide space in its branches for agents to sell insurance products. It takes the skills of a diplomat and the cunning of a guerrilla to strike deals that will serve your strategic ends and satisfy your partner's interests as well. Recall in this regard the example of Paine Webber, the brokerage house, and the alliance it forged with State Street Bank and Trust Company of Boston to gain access to the Visa International automatic teller network.

Citicorp, the largest U.S. bank-holding company, used similar SIS alliances to support its nationwide market expansion strategy. It contracted with Mpact, a bank-owned automated teller network based in Texas, and with Publix and Safeway, supermarket chains in Florida and California, respectively, that have installed cash-dispensing machines in their stores. These SIS alliances form part of the distribution network supporting Citibank's Financial Account, a major element in its diversification effort. Combining an interest-paying checking account, money market deposit account, CDs, a personal line of credit, and discount brokerage services, this product offers Citibank credit cardholders (over 12 million in the United States at the end of 1983) with one-stop financial services 24 hours a day.

ALLIANCES: PRODUCT EXTENSION

Product extension alliances create new uses, markets, or applications for products based on information systems.

Under the leadership of Prime Minister Edward Seaga, Jamaica adopted a policy of encouraging technological ventures designed to reduce the island's dependence on low-profit crops like sugar and introduce products with high market value. When an Israeli entrepreneur saw a news report detailing President Reagan's support for Seaga's policies, he also noticed the lush foliage on the island. Within a month, the entrepreneur had sent someone to Jamaica to collect soil and water samples for testing.

The entrepreneur, Eli Tisona, identified an opportunity to develop an SIS product extension alliance with the Jamaican government. If the soil and water tests proved positive, Tisona could leverage Israeli-developed information system applications in the agricultural field. When the tests confirmed his hunch, Tisona negotiated an agreement with the government to lease 4,500 acres and formed a partnership, Jamaica Agro Products, to grow winter vegetables, bananas, ornamental flowers, and nursery shrubs.

Perforated plastic hoses run through 125 acres of melons to deliver exact amounts of water and fertilizer, individually, to each plant. An Israeli-developed minicomputer system makes this possible by controlling the opening and closing of valves connecting over 250 sources of water and nutrients, as well as an intricate series of underground sensors that send data to the mini. Just 15 months after the start of the venture, the partners declared the project a success.

As margins on traditional lending activities erode due to the increasing intensity of competition in the financial services industry and to fluctuating rates, banks seek new sources of profit. Certain fee-generating services, like training or health programs developed for their own employees, are now offered to other institutions. According to the senior vice president for planning at Chemical Bank, "the banks, if they want to remain at the center of the payment system, are going to have to develop innovative services. If the banks don't do it themselves, somebody else is going to do it. We want to provide that service, and we think we can make money off it."

Licensing information systems and services, some large money center banks have discovered, presents one of the most lucrative and promising alliance opportunities for new revenue. Chemical's Trust and Investment Division, for example, franchises Trust Link, a new program that delivers trust services to smaller banking institutions in the United States. Trust Link makes use of ChemLink, another computerized system providing cash management services (under license) to both domestic and international banks. For an investment of about $200,000, Chemical offers Pronto, its innovative home-computer banking system, to banks that can't afford a $10 million development effort. Even before introducing Pronto to its New York customers, Chemical had signed six licensees.

Taking advantage of information system–based economies of scope represents another kind of leveraging opportunity open to entrepreneurial organizations. Sears, Roebuck (see Chapter 4) and J. C. Penney, exploiting economies of scope derived from their nationwide computer and telecommunication networks for retail credit, have each formed fee-generating SIS alliances that enable other organizations to share their respective networks. J. C. Penney forged SIS alliances with Shell and Gulf. Penney benefits by collecting fee revenues, while the petroleum firms, by reducing credit card transaction costs, can offer more competitive prices for their products.

For another variant, consider the joint venture created by AT&T's information systems unit and United Technologies' building systems group. Each will contribute personnel, products, and capital to a new business targeted at office building developers and others who provide tenant services. The joint venture will enable tenants to sign up for a variety of information system–based products and services associated with computer processing, security, telecommunications, etc. It will also offer building owners automated systems to control elevators, heat, air conditioning, and other building operations. In effect, this SIS alliance reflects an attempt to create the intelligent building. A number of other joint ventures in this area have been announced recently, some between suppliers, others between suppliers and owners.

ALLIANCES: PRODUCT DEVELOPMENT

Product development alliances are formed by firms desiring to create new products based on information systems.

In 1982, Kroger Company—a supermarket chain with 1,200 food stores, 500 pharmacies, and 32 food-processing plants in 21 states—announced that it had begun selling insurance, money market funds, and IRAs in one of its stores. Behind the announcement, believed to be the first notice of a financial services operation in a supermarket (but not quite a financial services supermarket), was an SIS product development alliance with Capital Holding, an insurance company with assets of $3.8 billion.

The joint venture projected costs of about $2 million, a substantial chunk of which was used to develop an information system that would immediately compare a customer's current automobile and home insurance with the offerings at the supermarket. For Capital, the alliance represented an opportunity to move into another channel of distribution, different from the traditional agency route. For Kroger, the aim was the same as it is for any new specialty service offered by the chain. "It is a service the customers want, and we are in the business of serving customers," the president of Kroger said at the time the SIS alliance was formalized.

Elsewhere, the impetus is entrepreneurial. Liberty National Bank & Trust Company, Oklahoma's second largest bank, joined with an independent retailer to found a chain of automated gasoline stations called "Sav–A–Dollar." Having operated a network of automated teller machines, Liberty had the information system experience to develop software to link automated fuel pumps to the bank's computers. Customers with Liberty bank cards can use them at any station in the chain to pay for their purchases. Unlike credit card transactions, sales at Sav–A–Dollar are deducted immediately from the customer's account.

Property and casualty insurance companies like Fireman's Fund are locked in an intense battle to save their networks of independent insurance agents. Large insurers have made clear their intention of luring the top agencies by helping them to automate. Industry observers see a radical realignment of the whole distribution system, with consolidations driven by the need to cut increasing information-handling costs. Some believe that as many as 20,000 of the nation's 65,000 independent agencies will either merge, sell out, or leave the business over the next 10 years.

Fireman's Fund, along with other major insurers, spends heavily on agent automation programs. In 1982, for example, it bought over $100 million worth of minicomputers destined for agency offices. To further support this critical automation program, Fireman's acquired the ARC Automation Group, a software company that produces information system applications for agents. It had, in effect, identified a need for an SIS product development alliance.

While this move may help Fireman's gain an edge over other insurers with independent agents, so-called direct-writing insurers who sell insurance through the mail or through exclusive agents or sales representatives still have often decisive cost advantages. But strategic agency automation programs like the one initiated by Fireman's may slow or stem the market share erosion experienced in the past few years.

Merrill Lynch, on the other hand, opted to forge an SIS development alliance by purchasing a minority equity interest in Institutional Network Corp. (also known as Instinet), a firm that offers customers an information systems–based service that automatically executes stock trades without having to be matched with other trades in the traditional auction market. Merrill uses the system as the market for about 100 over-the-counter (OTC) stocks. Currently, Merrill makes the market for about 1000 OTC issues. Whether Merrill will move to trade New York Stock Exchange issues on Instinet is still an open question that rivals ought to watch closely. Indeed, some have already followed Merrill's lead by taking minority positions in Instinet.

The last example of an SIS development alliance is a joint venture involving 25 Japanese firms. "Only in Japan could a consortium like this work," said the president of the Pacific Telecommunications Council when the creation of a second Japanese telephone company, Dai-Ni Den-Den Kikaku Co. Ltd. (DDK), was announced. DDK is the only Japanese competitor of Nippon Telegraph and Telephone, the government-owned monopoly that became a privately held corporation in 1985. Among the participants in the DDK venture are leading Japanese businesses in such disparate fields as banking, electronics, printing, and international trade (e.g., Sumitomo Bank, Sony, Dai Nippon Printing, and Mitsui). DDK expects to sell data transmission products and services, many of which will be driven by information systems, in Japanese and international markets.

CASE REFERENCES

American Express   *Business Week*, July 25, 1983; *The New York Times*, September 27, 1983; *The Wall Street Journal*, August 12, 1983; September 27, 1983.

Applied Data Research   *Information Systems News*, May 14, 1984; October 1, 1984.

ARC Automation   *The Wall Street Journal*, November 9, 1982.

Artificial Intelligence   *Software News*, January 1984.

Blue Cross–Blue Shield (New York)   *Computerworld*, July 2, 1984.

Capital Holding   *The New York Times*, September 28, 1982.

Chase Manhattan   *The Wall Street Journal*, February 15, 1984.

Chemical Bank   *The Wall Street Journal*, July 25, 1983; Annual Report, 1982.

Citibank   *The Wall Street Journal*, March 29, 1984; May 4, 1984.

Computer Corporation of America   *Computerworld*, May 7, 1984; *Information Systems News*, November 28, 1983.

Computervision   *Computerworld*, August 22, 1983; May 7, 1984.

Comshare   *Computerworld*, January 9, 1984.

Continuum   *Computerworld*, August 22, 1983.

Crowntek   See Computer Corporation of America.

Cullinet Software   See Electronic Data Systems.

Dai Nippon Printing   See DDK.

DDK   *Communications Week*, May 21, 1984.

Dreyfus   *The Wall Street Journal*, February 15, 1984.

Safeway   See Mpact.

Shell   See J. C. Penney.

Software AG   See Applied Data Research.

Sony   See DDK.

Sumitomo Bank   See DDK.

United Technologies   See AT&T.

BIBLIOGRAPHY

Wiseman, Charles. "Securing Competitive Edge through Strategic Information System Alliances." *Strategic Management Planning*, April 1984.

8

Becoming Strategic

PREPARING THE GROUND

This final chapter presents practical guidelines for developing SIS (strategic information systems) vision and suggestions for applying the framework introduced in the last six chapters. To prepare the ground for the growth of SIS vision, whether in the conventional firm lacking it or in the one desiring to strengthen it, top management should affirm its belief in three principles. The first relates to the nature of the firm:

1. The general purpose of the firm is to organize the *use* of the resources at its disposal so that it can achieve its long-term profitability and growth goals.

The resources of the firm comprise its *material* (plant, equipment, land, raw materials, and other tangible things) and *human* (skilled, unskilled, clerical, technical, managerial, etc.) assets. Each resource can provide a variety of services to the firm depending on how it is used. Two firms with exactly the same material and human resources may be notably different because of the services performed by these resources—that is, because of the ways top management has decided to use its resources. The second principle covers the use of the firm's resources.

2. The range of possible *uses* of the resources at the firm's disposal is limited only by the experience, knowledge, and imagination of its employees.

As a corollary to Principle 2, it follows that even at full capacity, when all resources are employed, there exist an almost unlimited number of services these resources could perform but are not performing because management has opted for one particular resource-use configuration from the infinite set open to it. The mere magnitude of possibilities should stimulate an enterprising management group to research alternative uses of its resources. For a different configuration might produce greater profit and growth than the current one.

It therefore pays to learn as much as possible about resources currently deployed and about their known alternative uses. Imaginative employees can, if properly motivated, be counted on to discover new uses for "dedicated" resources—materials, machines, or people—with which they are familiar. Some of these uses may promise greater benefits than those derived by the firm from its current deployment.

The third principle highlights the role of the firm's entrepreneurs, its agents of change:

3. Entrepreneurs are responsible for identifying new, productive *uses* of the resources at the firm's disposal.

The ideas of entrepreneurs bound the strategic-opportunity space open to the enterprising firm. Their contributions relate, in Penrose's words, "to the introduction and acceptance on behalf of the firm of new ideas, particularly with respect to products, location, and significant changes in technology, to the acquisition of new managerial personnel, to fundamental changes in the administrative organization of the firm, to the raising of capital, and to the making of plans for expansion, including the method of expansion."

Entrepreneurs fall into two classes: garden variety and empire builders. The garden variety, according to Penrose, directs its talents

> toward the improvement of the quality of their products, the reduction of costs, the development of better technology, the extension of markets through better service to customers, and the introduction of new products in which they believe their firms have a *productive* or *distributive advantage*. They take pride in their organization, and from their point of view the "best" way to make profits is through the improvement and extension of the activities of this organization. [Italics added.][21]

The empire builders, on the other hand, take delight not so much in garden-variety improvements as in radical departures from business as usual, reflected typically in the strategic thrusts of growth, alliance, and innovation. Empire builders seek opportunities to grow via vertical integration, to eliminate competitors by acquiring them, to build full-line businesses, and so on. (Nothing I have said should be construed as precluding the same person from providing entrepreneurial services, possessing strategic vision, or being part of the top management team.)

By accepting the three principles just discussed, the top management team affirms its commitment to change and to the agents of change, the firm's entrepreneurs. This commitment is a necessary condition for the development of SIS vision: it prepares the ground. SIS vision dictates *change*, envisioning as it does new *uses for information systems resources*—material or human, internal or external—as it charts the firm's strategic course.

"It is difficult to tell the short-sighted man how to get somewhere," the philosopher Wittgenstein observed "because you can't say to him: 'Look at the church tower 10 miles away and go in that direction.' " But fitted with the proper glasses, even the short-sighted can discern possible paths to follow. The last six chapters, as it were, ground the strategic lenses—glasses are now available to see new information systems and directions—to exercise SIS vision.

DEVELOPING COMPETITIVE STRATEGY

The process of developing a competitive strategy involves three steps: (1) assessing current policies and position, (2) determining environmental factors affecting the business, and (3) formulating a strategy to meet anticipated challenges over the planning period. The systematic search for SIS should be conducted within this context. Only then can the business unit be sure that it has comprehensively explored all options for using its information systems strategically. At each step in the process, SIS opportunities may be uncovered.

The competitive strategy process, as Derek Abell and others suggest, begins in Step 1 above by establishing a working definition of the unit's business, which captures the current scope of its activities and shows how it differentiates itself across segments and from its competitors. By analyzing the unit's products and markets, one can pin down scope in terms of customer groups targeted, customer needs satisfied, and technologies employed.

For example, a manufacturer of automatic teller machines (ATMs) may define its business as the production, distribution, and maintenance of ATMs that:

- Permit cash withdrawals, deposits, and checking/saving account transfers (customer needs).
- Serve banks in the United States and Canada (customer groups).
- Use 5-line display terminals with numerical keys linked via AT&T lines to a mainframe computer (technologies employed).

Another manufacturer may decide on a different definition by varying the values of the three scope variables. It may, for example, provide ATMs for the international marketplace and not limit itself to banks. Second, it may supplement the services offered at the machine to include stock market quotations, weather reports, stock and money fund transactions, and the like. Or it may offer a technologically unique product with voice response and activation capabilities.

With a working definition of the business, one can specify the product (industry, value-added) chain associated with it and identify the firm's strategic targets (i.e., its suppliers, customers, and competitors) that its thrusts (i.e., differentiation, cost, innovation, growth, and alliance) aim at. Strategists, it should be noted, tend to follow the "ready–aim–fire" rule rather than the more immediately satisfying "ready–fire–aim" command others often issue.

Good aim presupposes an understanding of the strengths and weaknesses of strategic targets, the threats and opportunities posed by them, and the firm's strategies to deal with them. This can only be acquired through careful analysis of the firm's suppliers, customers, and competitors, performed prior to the fashioning of strategic thrusts.

Supplier analysis. By examining the firm's value-added chain, the analyst can derive a list of suppliers. Items purchased should then be classified according to their *profit impact* and *supply risk*. An item may be classed as having high profit impact if, for instance, it is purchased in large quantity, its cost represents a sizable fraction of the total cost of purchased items, and its presence enhances the quality and growth prospects of the firm's product. It may be classed as having *high supply risk* if, for example, its availability is limited, few concerns offer it, demand from competitors who need it is high, and substitutes are expensive.

Figure 8-1   Categories of purchased items

Profit Impact

		High	Low
High	Supply Risk	Strategic	Bottleneck
Low		Leverage	Noncritical

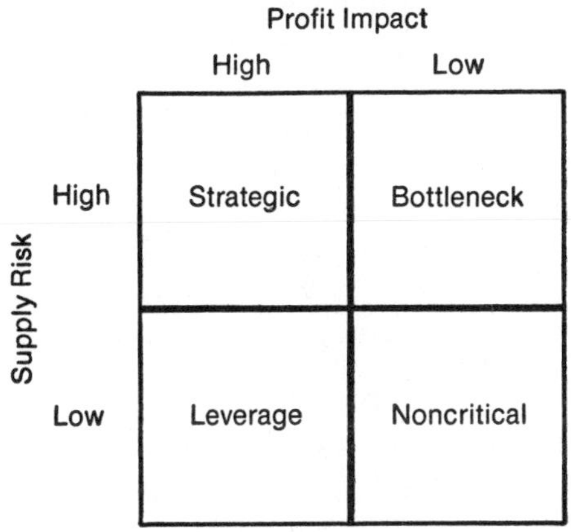

Using this schema, the firm can distinguish four categories of purchased items (see Figure 8–1): *strategic* (high profit impact, high supply risk), *bottleneck* (low profit impact, high supply risk), *leverage* (high profit impact, low supply risk), and *noncritical* (low profit impact, low supply risk).

After classifying purchased items in terms such as the above, the firm can calculate its bargaining power vis-à-vis its suppliers, category by category, by weighing such factors as:

Capacity utilization (if supplier's capacity is underutilized, its bargaining power may be diminished).

Break-even points (if supplier A's break-even point is set at 60 percent of capacity and B's at 75 percent, negotiations with A may be more difficult than with B).

Product differentiation (if supplier's product is highly differentiated, its bargaining powers may be quite high).

Volume purchase (if the firm purchases large volumes of a supplier's product, the firm's bargaining power may provide it with the leverage it needs to force a price reduction).

Information impactedness (if the firm is ignorant about the supplier's activities and product, the latter may act opportunistically and therefore wield great bargaining power over the firm).

Rating its strength vis-à-vis suppliers with respect to a particular item, the firm can, as Peter Kraljic suggests, "identify areas of opportunity or vulnerability, assess supply risks, and derive basic *strategic thrusts* for these items" [italics added]. At this point in the supplier analysis process, the firm should explore SIS opportunities, using the strategic option generator (see Chapter 2.)

Customer analysis. By examining the firm's value-added chain, the analyst can also identify buyers of its products. These buyers, like the suppliers, should be classified into various segments, with each isolating a well-defined set of customer benefits and characteristics. The firm's strategic marketers can then divine what these benefits ought to be and who should need or desire them. A customer analysis should address such questions as:

Why do customers buy?
When do they buy?
How much do they purchase?
Who makes the purchasing decision?
What information do customers require before purchasing?
Do they require any technical services?

Educational services?

Postsale services?

How do they use the product?

What can they tell us about competitive products?

Why should they select our product rather our rival's?

What factors may change the customer's purchasing behavior?

Where do they stand on price-quality trade-offs?

How loyal are they?

Will they switch from a rival's product to ours?

Can they make the product we're offering?

How much do they know about our activities?

These questions in no way exhaust the possibilities. Customer analysis strives to establish a reliable base of information for shaping strategic initiatives. After performing a customer analysis, the firm should be in a good position to evaluate its relative bargaining power vis-à-vis each of its customer groups and to devise strategic thrusts beamed at them. As in the supplier analysis process, the firm should at this point explore SIS opportunities, using the strategic option generator.

Competitor analysis. Rivals should be appraised comparatively—the firm versus a competitor, or the firm versus a group of competitors pursuing similar strategies—along dimensions such as the following:[22]

Function (R&D, manufacturing, marketing, distribution, information, finance, sales, service).

Organization (flat versus hierarchical, centralized versus decentralized, independent versus business unit of a conglomerate).

Culture (beliefs and expectations about innovation, decision making, exchange of ideas, and the like).

Human resources (skills and experience of top management, technical staff, etc.).

Product (quality versus price, wide versus narrow line, differentiated versus standardized, etc.).

After rating each factor (e.g., Is the competitor in an inferior, superior, or equal position vis-à-vis the firm with respect to R&D capabilities, distribution channel strength, product quality, etc.?), the firm should ascertain the source (if any) of the advantage or disadvantage.

Strategists may, from time to time, find it illuminating to identify *empathetically* with selected rivals, to imagine what it would be like to be in their position. Supported by data drawn from a *strategic intelligence system*—which presumably represents the distillate of annual reports, SEC documents, newspaper clippings, magazine articles, product comparisons, industry journals, consultant's studies, patent files, reports from suppliers, customers, other competitors, internal staff members, informal comments, and the like—the imaginative strategist can piece together a definition of the rival's business, a statement of its policies in relation to suppliers, customers, and competitors, and a summary of its main strategic thrusts.

This imagined world, consistent with the available empirical data, can be the starting point for a number of strategic probes on such subjects as possible responses of the rival to the firm's new offerings, to price changes, to new customer services, and to new alliances. Knowledge of the rival's organization, culture, human resources, and expected responses to strategic thrusts increases the chances of designing a thrust to exploit the rival's weaknesses and gain an edge for the firm. Just as the firm should explore SIS opportunities in supplier and customer analyses when strategic thrusts are considered, it should do the same in competitor analysis, again with the aid of the strategic option generator.

After assessing current policies and position in Step 1 of the competitive strategy development process, the strategist should forecast in Step 2 trends in *environmental variables* (economic, social, political, demographic, and governmental) affecting the firm's operations. This process, too, should stimulate the search for SIS openings. A trend of increased governmental regulation may prompt the design of an information system to cut through the bureaucratic morass slowing the introduction of new products. In the drug industry, for example, several firms with information systems are today in a position to secure formidable preemptive advantage over their rivals. So formidable is this advantage that it is currently being challenged in a court case.

Alternatively, an *industry analysis* may reveal SIS opportunities. By studying the $4 billion fragmented junkyard (i.e., automotive salvage) industry, for example, an analyst may uncover consolidation opportunities. The industry already uses computers to handle inventory, to aid in purchase decisions made at salvage auctions, and to prevent loss of sales because salespeople don't know whether a part is in stock.

An entrepreneurial firm may discover an opportunity to build a national service company to stock, locate, and deliver used parts to any U.S. city within 24 hours. Insurance adjusters who make 50 to 70 million requests a year for parts would certainly be eager customers for such a service, a service that could never become operational without information systems.

After completing Steps 1 and 2, the firm constructs, in Step 3, strategic programs to exploit its strengths or the weaknesses of its rivals, to defend against expected environmental threats and anticipated moves of competitors, and so on. Again, by examining these strategic programs, the enterprising firm may find occasions to use information systems to support or shape strategic thrusts associated with them.

From the above discussion, several conclusions may be drawn: First, the systematic search for SIS opportunities should be conducted within the context of competitive strategy development. Only then can the business unit be sure that it has canvassed all options.

Second, the hunt for SIS opportunities and threats demands the active participation of *information management* professionals. Creating advantages based on information systems consumes scarce resources, so it is best to engage the professionals as early and as intensively as possible. In my experience, the rewards have invariably exceeded the costs.

Third, the implementation of competitive strategies supported or shaped by any but the most primitive information systems requires close coordination between the business and technology groups. In addition, to avoid misallocations of resources, mistakes in setting priorities, and delays in systems delivery that may well jeopardize its competitive position, the business unit should synchronize its strategy with the information management group's *information systems plan*. To achieve this kind of alignment is usually not a perfunctory matter. The business unit often must take measures to reduce the noise levels that have for years inhibited communication between line and information system managers. This book, I hope, can be of some help in overcoming these communication problems, as it speaks in a language easily grasped by both groups.

MANAGING INFORMATION SYSTEMS STRATEGICALLY

The existence of SIS, a new variety of information system, should inspire the firm's information management (IM) function—today comprising not only computer operations but telecommunications and office automation as well—to reexamine its organizational obligations. Who within IM should be responsible for SIS identification and development? Should IM create a new group to handle SIS matters? Are new personnel attuned to the strategic perspective needed? If so, from where should they be recruited? Must IM change its approach to information systems planning (assuming it follows one) because of the emergence of SIS? These and similar questions should be addressed by IM's top managers once they have assimilated the strategic perspective on information systems. The following discussion should aid their deliberations. It covers two areas within which questions such as the above may be tackled: redefining the IM business and information systems planning.

Redefinition of the IM business.   To a large extent, the perspective one adopts on information systems predetermines not only what information systems are countenanced but also one's view of the IM function itself. In this section, I shall point out some of the organizational consequences of seeing the world through conventional glasses and show how the strategic perspective offers, at least for planning purposes, a viable alternative.

The conventional viewpoint, perhaps best represented by IBM's now classical guidelines for managing the IM function,* recommends that one

> analyze the management of the information resource from the enterprise or general management view. During this analysis, the guiding principle should be that data can be shared, that many demands are made of the data processing organization to produce applications, and that resources are limited.
>
> General management is concerned with *planning for and controlling* the data resource. Therefore, the IRM review should concentrate on recommending a *planning and control* function that will maximize the use of the resource, and insure that the recommended information architecture is implemented expeditiously. [Italics added.][23]

IBM groups IM activities, when viewed as a business, under three basic processes, reflecting Robert Anthony's planning and control paradigm (see Appendix A):

Strategic (e.g., information systems (I/S) strategic planning and control, architecture definition).

Tactical (e.g., data planning, systems planning).

Operational (e.g., project scheduling, change control).

To handle this "holy trinity," IBM recommends structuring the IM organization into four functional groups:

Data and application planning and control (e.g., I/S architecture, standards).

---

*Instead of *IM*, IBM prefers the term *information resource management* (IRM).

Data administration (e.g., logical data design, backup).

Application development (e.g., maintenance projects, information center).

Data processing and communications (e.g., networking, security).

IBM believes that its view of the IM function is "useful in analyzing the organizational and personnel skills necessary to properly manage, that is, *plan and control*, the information resource and data processing function" [Italics added].

As the above sketch suggests, the conventional perspective on information systems leads to a conventional view of the IM function. Just as the former focuses on conventional systems tied to the firm's planning and control processes, the latter (consistently enough) concentrates on IM planning and control processes intended to manage the firm's data resources efficiently.

If, as IBM claims, "general management is concerned with planning for and controlling the data resource," then shouldn't IM management also be concerned? Shouldn't it organize its activities according to technical specialities (such as those mentioned above) related directly to the resource to be planned for and controlled?

Perhaps. But it is not at all clear that general management's primary IM concern should be with the planning and control of the firm's data resources. In some enterprises, it may be; in others, perhaps not. Since it is obviously an open question, why should the IM function, a priori, organize itself and conceptualize its responsibilities in planning and control terms? Moreover, the planning and control mentality—which seems to characterize best the minds of the firm's bean counters rather than the thoughts of its entrepreneurs—reflects a passive, reactive, bookkeeping attitude. Bean counters plan and control. Entrepreneurs assume the risks associated with strategic thrusts with information systems used to support or shape them.

To encourage the discovery and implementation of SIS opportunities, IM needs to redefine its business from the strategic perspective. It needs to emphasize its products, customer groups, and customer needs as much as, if not more than, it does its technology and planning and control processes. Once it does this, IM should redefine its mission, at least for planning purposes, along customer and product line dimensions rather than along the conventional technical axis. In sum, I am proposing that IM needs to alter its management perspective to see itself as running a multidivisional, product-oriented business instead of operating a vertically integrated, technology-driven company.

To conceive of how the strategic perspective on IM might be implemented organizationally, assume that management information systems (MIS), management support systems (MSS), and SIS constitute product lines. These might be folded under an IM divisional head for information systems. The directors of MIS, MSS, and SIS would then be responsible for defining their "IM business units" in terms of customer groups served, customer needs satisfied, technologies employed, and so on. Each unit would organize itself into functional departments suitable to its product line and would develop strategies and programs to deal with its various constituencies. It would be no more surprising to find different cultures, organizational patterns, or kinds of personnel in each of these units than it would to discover such differences in any three businesses with products meeting different customer needs or supplying different market segments, yet in some cases, sharing technology.

Information systems planning. Narrowly defined, the term *information systems planning* signifies the planning required to develop a single computer application. This might involve such activities as defining the requirements of the application, designing the program, and allocating the proper resources for development. But the term has a wider sense in which it means the planning undertaken by an organization when it seeks to determine its information systems requirements *globally* and *systematically* so that it can prepare to meet its short- and long-term needs. I use the term here in the latter sense.

An information systems planning *methodology* is a valuable tool that an organization can use when conducting its study. A general-purpose planning methodology attempts to identify all the information system application opportunities that would satisfy the firm's needs; a special-purpose methodology focuses on particular kinds of information systems.

The two best known conventional information systems planning methodologies developed over the past 20 years are IBM's *business systems planning* (BSP) and MIT's *critical success factors* (CSF). BSP purports to be a general-purpose approach, emphasizing MIS. But it excludes explicitly the systematic search for SIS opportunities (see Appendix A for more details on this topic). CSF dedicates itself to the discovery of MSS, that is, decision support and executive information systems.

Extending now the proposal advanced in the last section, I suggest that the IM business units responsible for information systems adopt methodologies suited to their missions. The MIS group might use BSP, while the MSS group employs CSF.

But planning for SIS, on the other hand, requires a joint effort on the part of line or top management and the staff of the SIS unit. It should be an integral part of the firm's competitive strategy development process as sketched in the second section of this chapter. If no formal process exists, the joint team should gather enough data on the firm's suppliers, customers, competitors, products, and the like, so that it can understand the current strategic directions and what to expect in the future. SIS staff members could, among other things, contribute assessments of the information system's capabilities and of the firm's strategic targets, and forecasts of trends in the information processing industry.

GETTING STARTED

Members of three groups should possess SIS vision: top management, line management, and information management. Top management needs SIS vision because their task is to set the firm's strategic direction. Line management needs it because their functions are in closest contact with the firm's strategic targets. Information management needs it because they must assess the strategic significance of new technologies and trends in information processing and telecommunications. Of course, the enterprise should be open to any suggestions for SIS applications. But, in general, the firm's SIS entrepreneurs will be drawn from the three groups just mentioned. They are in a position to see opportunities and to act upon them.

Suppose the firm forms a task force, with members drawn from these three groups, to investigate the possibilities of SIS systematically. What should the members of this team know? Essentially, they should be familiar with the firm's competitive strategy, its information system capabilities, and the strategic perspective on systems, which implies an awareness (conscious or unconscious) of the theory of strategic thrusts and the strategic option generator (see Chapter 2).

Knowing who should possess SIS vision and what they should be taught is relatively straightforward. But how the strategic perspective should be introduced is another matter. Should it come through the front door (top management), the side door (line management), or the back door (information management)? Should the messenger be a member of the organization, a consultant, or a vendor selling products that could be part of an SIS? Or should there be a messenger team composed of members of these groups? Clearly, there is no best path for all to follow. Everything depends on local conditions. Rather than give a set of general suggestions, let me sketch three situations that I'm familiar with. These are cases in which ingredients of the strategic perspective on information systems entered the organizational bloodstream and started the development of SIS vision.

One vendor introduced the strategic perspective on information systems as a part of its three-day account manager conferences. These are held four or five times a year for 15–20 selected, high-performing sales personnel. Outsiders are invited to give presentations along with the firm's senior executives. Among recent topics covered were "The Microcomputer Perspective," "Managing End-User Computing," "A New Age in Information Systems," and "Strategic Information Systems." During the SIS session, discussion centered on possibilities for particular accounts and steps the vendor must take to encourage its clients to develop SIS vision.

In cases like this, vendors of products related to SIS (e.g., computer manufacturers, software producers, telecommunication suppliers) who understand the strategic perspective on information systems may provide the message directly to their customers. Or they may arrange for their customers to hear it, not from their mouths but from the voice of an independent presenter who has no ties to the vendor.

From a vendor's point of view, this is value-added marketing, aimed at differentiating the firm's product from those of the competition. From the customer's standpoint, it is a benefit that can result in a definite advantage. Both parties are therefore ideal candidates to participate in the dissemination of SIS vision.

A *Fortune* 20 user organization, on the other hand, moved to develop its SIS vision without any vendor prompting. Under a new corporate mandate to encourage "intrapreneurship"—that is, internal entrepreneurial activities—the information management group created a unique educational program.

Initiated in 1983, it is a 10-day residential program, run about eight times a year, with an assorted staff of internal and external speakers. The program encourages interaction, emphasizes the team approach, and draws on company-developed case studies. Originally targeted for the firm's over 1,000 information processing professionals, it plans to extend its audience to the end-user community as well.

Limited to 20–25 attendees, each session attempts to satisfy the seminar's ambitious objectives, which include the following:

- Provide an opportunity for computing professionals to increase their business awareness and strategic approach to systems solutions.
- Provide technology updates from a company perspective.
- Establish a climate where appropriate technical innovation and risk is encouraged.
- Provide an opportunity for members of different operating units to learn about each other and each other's environment.

Recent sessions included two- to four-hour modules presented by outside experts on "Technology Directions," "Telecommunications: Connecting People, Places, and Things," "The Changing Office," "Risk and Creativity," "Information System Accountability," "Managing the New Environment," and "Strategic Information Systems."

At the end of one SIS session, after a morning of theory and workshops, two participants rushed off before lunch to make a telephone call to the firm's executive vice president, the person who had been encouraging intrapreneurs to express their ideas across departmental boundaries or organizational levels. These two systems analysts saw an opportunity to develop an SIS that they believed could have a significant competitive impact on the firm's operations.

While the preceding two cases are instructive, I have saved for the last the most striking example of getting started, of becoming strategic. It depicts an organization that transformed its perspective on information systems from the conventional to the strategic within three months.

In the spring of 1983, the manager of a divisional information systems planning group for a large, diversified firm selling technological goods and services attended an all-day session on the strategic uses of information systems. It was a dress rehearsal for a series of public seminars on this subject. When the seminars were launched a few months later, the manager sent one of his staff members.

The consultant who presented the material heard nothing from these two attendees for 14 months. When he did, it was a request to present an in-house session to members of the divisional information management group. This group, he was told, would consist of the director of technological planning, directors of systems planning, and liaison analysts responsible for determining the information systems needs of the division's business units. In all, a total of 20–25 would attend the three-day, off-site seminar-workshop.

The seminar-workshop, run under the auspices of the planning group, had two objectives:

- To introduce the strategic perspective on information systems.
- To stimulate the imaginations of the attendees so that they would generate ideas about possible SIS opportunities.

But there was also an unstated goal: to build commitment to the SIS concept group by group. If the first sessions were productive, the show would go on the road in an attempt to win adherents in other organizational units.

Before the first off-site meeting, the divisional planners met with the consultant to discuss the agenda. They decided to have the consultant present his material on the first day. The following two days, to be run by the planners, would be devoted to brainstorming for SIS opportunities, with research provided by the staff on the company's strategic targets, competitive strategy, and so on. As the meeting broke, the consultant, curious about why he had been called more than a year after initial contact, was told that this was a high-priority project. Why? Because the divisional president, after reading a report by the IM planning head on SIS, decided to explore this virgin territory.

The off-site meeting brainstormed over 100 SIS ideas, 40 of which were picked for further analysis. The first group was sold. Two weeks later, at a meeting hosted by the divisional planners and attended by their counterparts and senior IM staff members from the business units, additional opportunities were uncovered. And another group was on board.

A week later, the consultant received another call from the divisional planning manager. "We need your services again," he was told, "this time for the corporate business planning group." It seems that the divisional president, after reviewing the results obtained from the two information management–sponsored sessions, met with the corporate operations group to marshall resources for the implementation of these SIS opportunities.

The consultant spent half a day explaining the strategic perspective to the corporate business planners. When he left the session, the divisional information systems planners took over. Their aim was to involve this new group in the process of SIS idea generation. For they knew that commitment down the line required involvement up front. They weren't disappointed. New ideas were generated; a third critical group bought in.

Two weeks after this session, the consultant was again called. This time, the assistance desired was not for a presentation to a new group but for a review of SIS projects already discovered and for additional suggestions based on the consultant's extensive file of SIS applications.

Within three months, this large, relatively slow-moving firm was up to speed on the strategic perspective on information systems, due to the combined efforts of corporate, line, and information management. It was moving systematically for the first time to use information systems resources and those of its allies strategically. It now possessed a portfolio of SIS opportunities tied to strategic thrusts and designed to gain competitive advantage.

If this book serves its purpose, it will awaken those now asleep to the threats and opportunities posed by information systems and inspire them to develop an SIS vision for meeting these inevitable challenges.

BIBLIOGRAPHY

Abell, Derek. *Defining the Business*. Englewood Cliffs, N.J.: Prentice-Hall, 1980.

Abell, Derek, and John Hammond. *Strategic Market Planning*. Englewood Cliffs, N.J.: Prentice-Hall, 1979.

Brand, William K., Robert Christian, and James Hulbert. "The Planning Process." 1980.

Hax, Arnoldo C., and Nicolas S. Maljuf. *Strategic Management: An Integrative Perspective*. Englewood Cliffs, N.J.: Prentice-Hall, 1984.

Hofer, Charles, and D. Schendel. *Strategic Formulation: Analytical Concepts*. St. Paul, Minn.: West Publishing, 1978.

IBM. *Information Systems Planning Guide: Business Systems Planning*. 3d ed. 1981.

Kanter, Rosabeth Moss. *The Change Masters: Innovation for Productivity in the American Corporation*. New York: Simon & Schuster, 1983.

Kraljic, Peter. "Purchasing Must Become Supply Management." *Harvard Business Review*, September–October 1983.

MacMillan, Ian. "Seizing Competitive Initiative." *Journal of Business Strategy*, Spring 1982.

MacMillan, Ian, and Patricia Jones. "Designing Organizations to Compete." *Journal of Business Strategy*, Spring 1984.

Montgomery, David, and Charles Weinberg. "Toward Strategic Intelligence Systems." *Journal of Marketing*, Fall 1979.

Penrose, Edith T. *The Theory of the Growth of the Firm*. Oxford: Basil Blackwell, 1959.

Porter, Michael. *Competitive Strategy*. New York: Free Press, 1980.

Rockart, John. "Chief Executives Define Their Own Data Needs." *Harvard Business Review*, March–April 1979.

Schwartz, Howard, and Stanley Davis. "Matching Corporate Culture and Business Strategy." *Organizational Dynamics*, Summer 1981.

Wittgenstein, L. *Culture and Value*. Trans. Peter Winch. Chicago: University of Chicago, 1980.

A

Conventional Perspective

INTRODUCTION

To understand the conventional perspective on information systems and to appreciate the hold it has had for almost the past 30 years, one needs to examine its roots and the conceptual landmarks that have sustained it. These sources of growth reflect intellectual efforts made by a tightly knit community dedicated to explicating the fundamental concepts of information systems.

From this examination, a coherent pattern emerges. The conventional perspective, I shall show, is based on Robert Anthony's paradigm (model, theory) for planning and control systems, developed in 1965 and applied in the information management field by William Zani in 1970. Zani's work spotlighted areas in need of more penetrating analysis. In the 70s and 80s, academics and others working on the conceptual foundation of information systems explored in greater depth topics merely mentioned in passing by Zani. Anthony Gorry and Michael Scott Morton and Peter Keen focused on systems designed especially for managerial decision making; Richard Nolan, IBM planners William King and John Rockart concentrated on information systems planning topics; Rockart and Michael Treacy specialized in systems targeted for top managers.

In each of these explorations, and in countless others undertaken by members of the rapidly expanding band of information management professionals, Anthony's paradigm looms large. For these are the efforts of community members to articulate the planning and control model.

After describing Anthony's paradigm, I shall trace its application in the information management field and its articulation in three of the most important information systems areas: decision support systems, executive information systems, and information systems planning. These are critical areas because they guide the methodical search for information system investment opportunities and determine the allocation of an organization's scarce system development resources.

ANTHONY'S PARADIGM

Professor Robert Anthony's *Planning and Control Systems: A Framework for Analysis,* still available in 1984, has gone through almost a dozen printings since its publication in 1965. Its success confirms the prescient opinion of Bertrand Fox, the former director of research at the Harvard Business School, who wrote in the Foreword to the first edition:

> This statement of a conceptual framework for the study of planning and control systems can be expected to have an important effect on later analytical studies undertaken at the school. The basic purpose of this volume is not to report research findings themselves but to set forth a framework which will influence the conduct of research in the broad area of planning and control systems.

When the book appeared, at least two of Anthony's colleagues were using the framework in research projects, and several graduate students had incorporated it into their dissertations. Anthony himself hoped that his conceptual grid would aid not only researchers and students but also those who designed and used such systems.

In the past 20 years, Anthony's schema has achieved paradigm status, taking root first in the soil of management planning and control and spreading later to adjacent fields as well. Before tracing its application and articulation in the information management area, I shall highlight its salient features.

Prior to proposing the framework, it appears that Anthony viewed the realm of planning and control systems in much the same ways as a thoroughbred handicapper with an analytical bent might see his chosen domain—as one in which there are "scarcely any generally accepted principles, and everyone in the field, therefore, works by intuition and folklore."

But unlike the handicapper, Anthony addressed a field amenable to analytical persuasion. To reduce its intellectual chaos, he proposed a framework that has become, for some, the "holy trinity" of planning and control:

- *Strategic planning:* The process of deciding on objectives of the organization, on changes in those objectives, on the resources used to attain those objectives, and on the policies that are to govern the acquisition, use, and disposition of those resources.
- *Management control:* The process by which managers assure that resources are obtained and used effectively and efficiently in the accomplishment of the organization's objectives.
- *Operational control:* The process of assuring that specific tasks are carried out effectively and efficiently.

According to Anthony these three processes tend to form a hierarchy, with strategic planning at the top and operational control at the bottom, along a variety of dimensions: *time* (long-range, medium-range, day-to-day), *organizational level* (top management, top and operating management, supervisory management), *degree of judgment* (great, some, none), *importance of decisions* (major, medium, minor), and so on.

Planning and control systems facilitate the processes with which they are associated; they are the means by which the processes occur. Such systems are intended to help managers make, implement, and control decisions. A strategic planning system designer, for example, might organize the process through which line managers work to resolve strategic issues. This should not be confused with a computer-based system (incorporating a model of the firm) used by strategic planners to explore alternative scenarios.

Strategic planning is the process of determining organizational objectives and policies. It is concerned with major decisions (e.g., diversification, acquisition, "resizing") having long-term consequences. Management control has to do with the ongoing operations of the enterprise, adhering as best it can to guidelines established through the strategic planning process. In operational control, the emphasis switches from more general issues to individual tasks and transactions: scheduling or controlling jobs through a shop, procuring certain items of inventory, and so on. Many of the activities subject to operational control are programmable—that is, capable of being formulated in terms of well-defined rules that could, in theory, be represented by a computer program.

The control aspects of strategic planning include top management's need to monitor staff progress on issues outstanding, to appraise the performance of those involved in the process, and to determine whether agreed-upon strategies are being implemented. This kind of control is usually neither systematic nor objective, since standards of comparison are difficult to formulate.

In the process of management control, line managers take center stage. Their judgments

> are incorporated in the approved operating plans, and they are the persons who must influence others and whose performance is measured. Staff people collect, summarize, and present information that is useful in this process, and they make calculations that translate management judgments into the numbers that appear on the budget. . . . The decisions, which are the important part of the whole process, are made by the line, not the staff.[24]

The focus of operational control differs substantially from the other two processes in the trinity. For one thing, "the system itself is a much more important part of the process," stating, as it often does, the action to be taken and sometimes even making the decision. "With a properly designed system, operational control will require a minimum of management intervention." But operational control systems are not necessarily simple or restricted activities. Production-scheduling systems for General Motors, for example, would involve worldwide networks of plants, parts, suppliers, and so on.

APPLYING ANTHONY'S PARADIGM

In "Blueprint for MIS," a six-page article perhaps best known for its broad scope, William Zani addresses the question, How should top management think about MIS? Appearing in the November–December 1970 issue of the *Harvard Business Review* (five years after Anthony's *Planning and Control Systems*), this brief piece represents the first widely circulated application of Anthony's paradigm in the information management field.

Zani, an assistant professor of business administration at the Harvard Business School, where he specialized in computer systems, was concerned about the failure of traditional MIS to meet the information needs of managers. As he saw it, most MIS were not designed according to a well-conceived plan but rather emerged, ad hoc, from the bowels of the business. They were spin-offs, by-products, that formed a "crazy quilt of residues from automated clerical procedures" and generated far more paper and frustration than valuable managerial information. If the long-heralded promise of MIS was to be realized, a new approach to information systems design was needed, a top-down method "to focus on the critical tasks and decisions made within an organization and to provide the kind of information that the manager needs to perform those tasks and make those decisions."

Zani's blueprint for improved MIS design centers on managerial decision making, on the problem of how to identify the information needs of managers. The only way to solve this problem, Zani suggests, is to isolate the organization's major decisions and the information they require. What are these decisions? Precisely the ones that fall within Anthony's holy trinity of planning and control processes.

Guided by an awareness of organizational objectives, strategy, and critical success factors, the Zanian information system designer analyzes the "company's decision-making patterns in strategic planning, management control, and organizational control." Through this process, the designer will uncover the organization's critical information needs and identify MIS opportunities to satisfy them.

Consider, for instance, the planning area. Zani claimed:

> The implications of corporate strategy for MIS design have largely escaped attention. Strategy should exercise a critical influence on information systems design. . . . If a company changes its strategy so

that its MIS focuses on factors no longer relevant—if now it urgently needs cash flow data, say, when it formerly needed sales data, then the system is no longer valuable. Strategy dictates firm, explicit objectives for systems design.[25]

Zani's views here are typical of conventionalists like King (see below) who believe that corporate strategy should determine system design objectives and that the organization's information systems plan should be aligned with its strategy. But with their vision channeled by the boundaries of Anthony's paradigm, they look only for system opportunities to support managerial decision making, opportunities falling exclusively within the holy trinity of planning and control processes. What they discern on the information system horizon is what they expect to find: conventional management support systems.

Zani recognizes the existence of two types of information system: (1) those automating clerical operations and (2) those supplying decision-making information to managers. He calls Type 2 "management information systems" and leaves Type 1 unnamed. In terms of my taxonomy, Type 2 should be understood as instances of management support systems and Type 1 as management information systems. This terminological discrepancy is a bit confusing because Zani wrote in 1970, before information systems varieties had been more clearly differentiated. (In 1971, Gorry and Scott Morton (see below) introduced a new framework in which Zani's MIS, following what was quickly becoming common usage, would be classed as decision support systems.)

DECISION SUPPORT SYSTEMS

In 1971, the Massachusetts Institute of Technology's *Sloan Management Review* published "A Framework for Management Information Systems," written by Gorry and Scott Morton. Both were faculty members at MIT and part of the growing information management community, the latter a recent graduate of the Har-

Scott Morton define DSS as information systems that support either semi- or unstructured decisions made in the areas of strategic planning, management control, and operational control. For them, "information systems should exist only to support decisions," and therefore, understanding managerial decision making "is a prerequisite for effective systems design and implementation."

Although Gorry and Scott Morton were the first to define this new species of information system, the promise of DSS wasn't realized until the late 70s and early 80s. Advances in information processing technology, coupled with the further expansion and dissemination of the DSS concept by Keen and Scott Morton in their 1978 book, *Decision Support Systems: An Organizational Perspective*, paved the way.

Keen and Scott Morton modified the original definition of DSS somewhat by restricting the decisions to be supported to the semistructured. But they continued to use Anthony's paradigm in their information system framework. They also made their characterization of DSS more concrete by pointing out four levels of support. DSS could provide (1) access to data, (2) filters for data selection and sorting, (3) simple calculations, comparisons, and projections, and (4) decision-making models. At each level, the system used is assumed to be, unlike the typical MIS, under the control of the manager.

Gorry and Scott Morton recognize the existence of two kinds of information systems: structured decision systems (roughly coextensive, they claim, with MIS) and decision support systems. They note that other kinds of computer applications including "straightforward data handling with no decisions" are possible, citing payroll as an example. Keen and Scott Morton, writing in 1978, observe that the term *MIS* "means different things to different people, and there is no generally accepted definition recognized by those working on the field." Data processing professionals, for instance (according to the authors), count "payroll and accounts receivable programs and other clerical data processing activities" as MIS.

In terms of the taxonomy introduced in Chapter 1, decision support systems are a species of management support systems;

vard Business School whose dissertation dealt with the subject
management decision systems. Aware as they must have been
Anthony's paradigm and Zani's application of it in the informati
management field, Gorry and Scott Morton, unlike their predec
sors, were concerned explicitly with *how* information syste1
could have a greater impact on managerial decision making.

To address this problem, they focused first on describing org
nizational activities in terms of the type of decision involved. Tl
done, they then proposed a new conceptual grid for screening co1
puter application opportunities. Whereas Zani had been content
suggest a better design approach to cope with the failure of MIS
fulfill their promise, Gorry and Scott Morton advocated a far mo
radical alternative, dividing information system opportunities in1
two distinct kinds: *structured decision systems*—which the
claimed encompassed "almost all of what has been called manag
ment information systems (MIS) in the literature—an area that h
had almost nothing to do with real managers or information bu
has been largely routine data processing" (e.g., accounts receiv
able, inventory control, and order entry)—and *decision suppor*
systems (DSS).

How, then, did Gorry and Scott Morton define DSS? At thi
point, the reader should not be surprised to learn that they ap
pealed to Anthony's holy trinity for support. But they did more
than this. They combined Anthony's paradigm with concepts introduced by Herbert Simon when he investigated the decision-
making process. For Simon, "decisions are *programmed* to the extent that they are repetitive and routine, to the extent that a definite
procedure has been worked out for handling them so that they
don't have to be treated de novo each time they occur. . . . Decisions are *nonprogrammed* to the extent that they are novel, unstructured, and consequential." Gorry and Scott Morton use
"structured" and "unstructured" in place of "programmed" and
"nonprogrammed" to avoid associations with computers and to encourage links to problem-solving activities.

By combining Anthony's holy trinity of management activities
and their own variations of Simon's decision types, Gorry and

structured decision systems and data handling applications are instances of management information systems.

EXECUTIVE INFORMATION SYSTEMS

In "The CEO Goes On-Line," published in the January-February 1982 issue of the *Harvard Business Review*, Rockart and Treacy announced "the emergence in a number of companies of a new kind of executive information support (or 'EIS') system." In a 1981 paper on this topic, "Executive Information Systems," they (like their intellectual progenitors, Zani and Gorry and Scott Morton) had voiced concern about the failure of existing systems to satisfy the information needs of managers. But by 1981, the reason for concern had switched from the inadequacies of MIS to the incompleteness of DSS.

Rockart and Treacy contend that the conceptual framework developed for DSS by Gorry and Scott Morton in 1971 and refined by Keen and Scott Morton in 1978 cannot be used to identify and explain the new, top executive uses of EIS. DSS, they argue, are for middle- and lower-level managers, those who make well-defined, repetitive decisions. For these corporate cogs, building a model that generates information to support such decisions is the goal. Top managers, on the other hand, are paid to deal with uncertainty, to make decisions today and tomorrow unlike decisions they made yesterday. For these executives, flexibility is the key. A capability to access data and manipulate it to their own ends with an easy-to-use computer language is essential.

Citing Ben Heineman, president and CEO of Northwest Industries (he spends a few hours a day at a computer terminal in his office retrieving reports on Northwest's business units and analyzing data with the help of an effective computer language), John Schonenman, chairman of the board and CEO of Wausau Insurance Companies (he sits at a terminal tapping into on-line data bases containing information about Wausau's operations and those of its competitors), and others as exemplary users of the new EIS,

Rockart and Treacy propose "a simple model of EIS structure and development into which fit all individual systems" they have observed.

Within their framework, an information system is an EIS if it possesses the following four features:

1. Central purpose: "The top executives who personally use computers do so as part of the *planning and control processes in their organization*. The provision of information to senior management for such purposes is certainly nothing new; the reason for EIS is to support a more effective use of this information." [Italics added.]
2. Information repositories: These are tailored, often idiosyncratic data bases containing detailed past, present, and future data—by business unit—on important business variables drawn, for example, from the general ledger, sales reports, and industry statistics.
3. Methods of use: "(a) For *access* to the current status and projected trends of the business and (b) for personalized *analyses* of the available data." [Italics added.]
4. Support organization: A group of consultants, or "EIS coaches," who provide ongoing assistance to the top executive user team.

Rockart and Treacy see the emergence of EIS as signaling a new era in the organizational use of computers. What they mean, evidently, is that more and more top managers and their staffs will use computers to access and analyze data contained in information repositories. But does this expanded use of computers constitute an organizational use radically different from former uses? The answer here, it seems, is no.

In the preceding paragraph, the word *use* is employed equivocally. What Rockart and Treacy mean by it is indicated by Item 3 above: that is, *use* of computers to access and analyze data. When I use the term *use*, I mean organizational role or purpose. In the jargon of Appendix B, Rockart and Treacy's "use" is equivalent to our "technical function." Their "central purpose" (see Item 1 above) is our "organizational use."

With the semantic fog lifted, EIS can be seen as instances of management support systems. What Rockart and Treacy tout as signs of a new era appear on inspection to be repackaged versions of systems reflecting Anthony's planning and control paradigm. If they differ from DSS (and here Keen and Scott Morton could offer good reasons for taking EIS as subspecies of DSS) they must be distinguished in terms of their targets and thrusts.

EIS are targeted at top managers and their staffs who engage in planning and control activities at the corporate office, business unit, or functional level of the organization. This emphasis on executive management is intended to differentiate EIS from DSS.

The conventional thrust of EIS is to supply top managers and their staffs with information to support the full range of their activities. On this description, EIS satisfy more than the decision-making needs of top managers. Using EIS, for example, may simply put an executive in a better position to understand the operations falling under his or her aegis.

The conventional perspective on information systems, as the above discussion indicates, offers six generic opportunity areas for the development of computer applications (see Figure A–1). This

Figure A–1 Opportunities for conventional information systems

	Conventional Target		
	Strategic planning	Management control	Operational control
Automating basic processes			
Satisfying information needs			

Conventional Thrust

perspective focuses attention on three targets (people or processes associated with strategic planning, management control, and operational control) and two thrusts (automating basic processes and providing information for decision making or other managerial or professional purposes). These conventional targets and thrusts should be contrasted with those related to SIS (see Figure 2–1).

INFORMATION SYSTEMS PLANNING

Narrowly defined, the term *information systems planning* signifies the planning required to develop a single computer application. This might involve such activities as defining the requirements of the application, designing the program, and allocating the proper resources for development. More commonly, however, the term is understood in a wider sense as meaning the planning undertaken by an organization when it seeks to determine its information systems requirements *globally* and *systematically*, so that it can prepare to meet its short- and long-term needs. I shall use the term in this latter sense unless otherwise indicated.

An information systems planning *methodology* is a valuable tool that an organization can use when conducting its study. A general-purpose planning methodology aims to identify all the information system application opportunities that would satisfy its needs; a special-purpose methodology focuses on a particular kind of information system, such as DSS or EIS, and aims to identify all such application opportunities that would satisfy the organization's needs.

One test of the adequacy of a methodology is its completeness. By this I mean: Are the steps in the process such that a planner trained in following them can identify and explain all and only the information system application opportunities the methodology intends to account for? A methodology is *complete* if the answer is yes. Otherwise, it is *incomplete*. If it is incomplete, this is cause for concern as it entails that there are applications the methodology cannot account for. This is a crippling defect in a general-purpose methodology; in a special-purpose approach, it is noteworthy only when the methodology fails to identify and explain instances of the kind of systems it purports to identify and explain. Certainly, we wouldn't want to hold a DSS methodology in contempt if it didn't identify MIS opportunities, and vice versa.

The above definitions prepare the ground for my analysis of the primary information systems planning approaches developed over the past 20 years. I have selected the most representative and best-known methodologies while recognizing that many have found other approaches to be of use in planning for information systems. In general, the core of these alternatives is reducible to, or an extension of, one or more of the representative methodologies. My aim here is not, however, to examine in detail the extant approaches to information systems planning. Rather, it is to show that Anthony's paradigm is central to each.

Nolan's Stage Methodology

Nolan's stage methodology, one of the best-known approaches to information systems planning, was formulated in the early 70s[26] and enhanced during the next decade when Nolan left his teaching post at the Harvard Business School and formed the consulting firm of Nolan and Norton, Inc. This is not the place to rehearse the specifics of the stage hypothesis. Roughly speaking, Nolan claims that organizations pass through various stages in their use of information processing technology. On the original hypothesis, he postulated four growth stages: initiation (computer acquisition), contagion (intense systems development), control (proliferation of controls), and integration (user/service orientation). In "Managing the Crises in Data Processing,"[27] he added two others—data administration and maturity—to account for organization behavior indicating a transition from the task of managing the computer to that of managing the data resource.

The stage hypothesis provides the basis for Nolan's information systems planning methodology, as each stage is characterized by certain benchmarks relating to information processing technology, data processing organization, user awareness, data processing planning and control, and the organization's portfolio of applications. By determining where an organization fits on the various benchmark scales and knowing when it ought to be at the next stage, a planner can use Nolan's approach to formulate programs that facilitate the transition from stage to stage.

To get the feel for this routine, consider the assessment of the application portfolio. Nolan proposes, first, that one "define the set of business functions for the organizational unit that represent cost-effective opportunities (e.g., manufacturing, marketing, distribution, finance, accounting, personnel, administration) to apply DP technology." He calls this the "normative applications portfolio." It represents "the business functions that would be receiving DP support if the company had achieved Stage 6 maturity." Second, take each function, and "indicate for each set of systems the support that data processing gives to the function in the organization." Third, he suggests using a 10-point scale to determine the support currently provided relative to what should be provided for the function. These assessments are then compared to Nolan's investment benchmarks for data processing applications: strategic planning, management control, and operational systems.

Strategic planning systems include those designed for economic forecasting, management planning, strategic and operating plans, and sales and profit planning. Management control systems include those designed for purchasing, inventory control and valuation, and market research. Operational systems include those designed for cash management, machine control, credit, payroll, general ledger, and stockholder relations.

Nolan's universe of information systems application opportunities seems to have been set in concrete back in the early 70s, at the time Anthony's paradigm was beginning to be articulated in the information management field. In "Plight of the EDP Manager"[28] Nolan draws a "basic map of opportunities for EDP applications" in the form of a triangle, horizontally trisected. In the top third are the application opportunities for senior management, in the middle third those for middle management, and in the bottom third those for operations. Recall from the description of Anthony's paradigm above that these levels correspond exactly to the holy trinity of planning and control processes: strategic planning, management control, and operational control. Nolan has modified Anthony's lowest level, from operational control to operations. This permits him to accommodate the operational systems like payroll that Anthony excluded from his taxonomy.

But the effect on an information systems planner's vision is essentially unchanged. The focus is still on internal operations, on automating basic processes or satisfying the decision maker's needs for information. Within each level, according to Nolan, there are areas where it is neither feasible nor economical to apply computers, and there are areas where computers can be used for operations processing and for generating reports for decision making. While recognizing that an organization's opportunities may be a bit more complex than his models, he claims that this "basic layout is generally valid."

From 1973 to 1978, Nolan's published views about the range of system opportunities remained unchanged. In his Spring 1983 letter to management, "Building the Company's Computer Architecture Tactical Plan," he extends the analysis of the application portfolio by adding a technological dimension. He continues to look at the planning, control, and operations functions, but now with respect to such information processing technologies as CAD/CAM, robotics, data processing, office automation, and personal computers. In terms of a planner's mental set of application opportunities, it's business as usual. Up to 1983 at least, Nolan's general-purpose approach to information systems is clearly incomplete, for it offers no guidelines for identifying or explaining SIS opportunities.

Critical Success Factors (CSF)

In "Chief Executives Define Their Own Data Needs,"[29] Rockart reported on a new approach to defining the information needs of top executives—CEOs and general managers. Developed by a research team at MIT's Sloan School of Management, the CSF method addresses the still-common complaint of managers about their information systems support—"too much and in general irrelevant."

The CSF approach homes in on individual managers and their information needs. Critical success factors for any business are defined as "the limited number of areas in which results, if they are satisfactory, will ensure successful competitive performance for the organization. They are the few key areas [three to eight] where things must go right for the business to flourish." In the supermarket industry, for example, they might include product mix, inventory, sales promotion, and pricing. "If results in these areas are not adequate, the organization's efforts for the period will be less than desired. . . . [CSFs] should receive constant and careful attention from management. The current status of performance in each area should be continually measured, and that information should be made available."

Rockart notes that the CSF concept, introduced by Daniel and picked up by Anthony and his colleagues, fits nicely into the planning and control framework. "That is, the control system must report on those success factors that are perceived by the managers as appropriate to a particular job in a particular company." For Rockart, "the CSF approach does not attempt to deal with information needs for strategic planning. Data needs for this management role are almost impossible to preplan. The CSF method centers, rather, on information needs for *management control* where data needed to monitor and improve existing areas of business can be more readily defined."

When the CSF concept was introduced by Rockart in 1979, its primary use was to help individual managers determine their information needs. It is now thought to be another tool, like IBM's BSP or Gibson and Nolan's stages, to guide organizations in the information systems planning process. In "A Primer on Critical Success Factors,"[30] Rockart and Bullen discuss how the CSF method can be used to identify the CSFs of individual managers; these "will indicate one or more key 'information data bases' or 'data processing systems' which should receive priority treatment in the information systems development process." Such key data bases are precisely the information repositories that support the development of executive information systems, systems designed to make information available to top executives for query and analysis.

We have come full circle. The CSF method, now used primarily as a special-purpose information systems planning approach, aims at identifying executive information systems opportunities. There is an admirable consistency here. Just as EIS are defined within the context of Anthony's paradigm, the CSF method also is rooted in the holy trinity of planning and control processes. It is a methodology dedicated to identifying and developing conventional information systems, at satisfying the information needs of an organization's top managers.

IBM's Business Systems Planning (BSP)

IBM's BSP, like Nolan's stage routine, is a general-purpose methodology for information systems planning. Its first and most important objective "is to provide an information systems plan that supports the business's short- and long-term information needs and is integral with the business plan." The importance of BSP in the information management field is due largely to IBM's supremacy in the computer industry. Thousands of customers have been introduced to the concepts of BSP through reading the various editions of IBM's *The Information Systems Planning Guide* (the Blue Book, 1975; the Pumpkin Book, 1978; the Green Book, 1981), attending executive presentations conducted at IBM education centers in Poughkeepsie, New York, and San Jose, California, and studying in formal training classes held at IBM locations around the world. Most of the other general-purpose approaches to information systems planning (e.g., Honeywell's *planning methodology*, Martin's information engineering, and those pushed by large accounting firms) are lineal descendants of BSP.

From IBM's viewpoint, BSP serves two purposes. First, it provides the marketing group with an opportunity to project what they believe to be the full range of systems a customer account could use. This helps marketing set sales goals for IBM hardware, software, and services. Second, it offers customers a chance to view their information management function globally, from the top down, and to determine the set of information and data bases required to support its operations.

My interest in BSP is pragmatic. Being the dominant methodology for identifying information systems application opportunities, its influence is widespread and deeply rooted. It reflects, perhaps more than any other process, the conventional perspective on information systems. Moreover, as BSP has evolved, it has incorporated elements of other planning approaches in an effort to adapt to changing needs.

IBM pictures BSP as a mechanism for translating an organization's business strategy into its information systems plan. This is an idea developed by King in "Strategic Planning for MIS"[31] and extended in his "Achieving the Potential of Decision Support Systems."[32] As King has it, MIS strategic planning is the process of mapping an organizational strategy set—consisting of the organization's objectives (e.g., to increase earnings by 10 percent per year), strategies (e.g., diversify into new businesses), and strategic attributes (e.g., sophisticated management)—into its MIS strategy set—consisting of MIS objectives (e.g., provide information on new business opportunities), constraints (e.g., system must provide reports involving various levels of aggregation), and design strategies (e.g., design on a modular basis).

Each element of the MIS strategy set is "derived" or "inferred" by an information analyst from the organizational strategy set. Thus, the MIS objective of "providing information on new business opportunities" is derived from the organizational strategy of "diversifying into new businesses," which in turn is related to such organizational objectives as "increasing earnings by 10 percent per year."

This process of strategy set transformation purportedly enables the organization to identify information systems that are closely related to its strategy. King believes that what he is proposing is a methodology for linking an organization's decision-supporting MIS (he still adheres to the term *MIS* rather than adopting the more fashionable *DSS*) and its goals and strategies. He sees his approach as

valid for the support of middle-level organizational decisions, a management level which Anthony has classified as the *management control* level. Moreover, the approach is even valid for an MIS which is designed to support strategic choice, since there must be some starting point at which a system is developed to feed back information on the validity and degree of attainment of strategies already chosen. [Italics added.][33]

King's work is of interest to us on two counts: first, because IBM has stamped its seal of approval on it; second, because it is symptomatic of the conceptual blindness induced by an almost religious belief in Anthony's holy trinity.

When King proposes to link information systems support directly to corporate strategy (a noble intention, to say the least) he sees only the support offered by applications that ply managers with decision-making information. Indeed, all the MIS objectives he derives from the sample organizational strategy set and which identify information system application opportunities relate exclusively to supplying timely, accurate, speedy *information* to managers.

Take the example given above concerning the organization's diversification strategy. King views this as implying a system that will "provide information on new business opportunities." This may be just what the CEO desired, but it reveals a narrow mental set that is incapable of conceiving another kind of organizational use for information systems. When Toys "Я" Us, for example (see Chapter 6), diversified into children's apparel, it used information systems developed for its toy business to propel its growth thrust. It saw opportunities to use information systems assets to shape its strategy. This kind of move would never occur to an information analyst using King's strategy-set transformation approach for identifying information system opportunities. If you're set on thinking about reports to management, you're probably blind to strategic opportunities like those that could transform your business.

Returning now to BSP, let us review how it defines the range of application opportunities open to an organization. Like Zani, Gorry and Scott Morton, Keen and Scott Morton, and Rockart and Treacy, IBM perceives the need for some reasonable framework in terms of which it can define information system opportunities. IBM proposes that "first, the emphasis in information systems should be in support of management decision making. This is in contrast to more traditional bookkeeping or record-keeping functions. Business decisions are made for various purposes, but most can be associated with either *planning* or *control*."

The stage has been set. Anthony's paradigm enters IBM's framework at this point in full force, with definitions of the holy trinity quoted.

Yet BSP doesn't stop here. It needs more than Anthony's paradigm to capture all the information system opportunities it seeks.

The vehicle for accomplishing this represents one of the most significant contributions made by BSP. To get at the myriad application opportunities lying outside Anthony's paradigm, BSP introduces the notions of *resource management* and *business process*. Every organization must manage such universal resources as people, facilities, materials, money, and information. The requirements dictated by these resources are in turn determined by the organization's product. This latter, having all the life-cycle attributes of the other resources, is known as the *key* resource.

> Each resource is managed through planning and control decisions of the three levels previously discussed. Resource management has the desired characteristic of cutting across organizational boundaries— vertically across management levels and horizontally across functional lines. Thus a framework based on resources as well as planning and control levels can be established, and an information system architecture can be applied within this framework.[34]

Business processes are the basic activities and decision areas of the organization, independent of reporting relationships or management responsibilities. BSP claims that a logical set of such processes can be defined for any business. Examples of business processes include: market planning (marketing research, forecasting, pricing, etc.), accounting (payroll, fixed asset, cost, cash management, etc.), financial planning and control (budgeting, managerial accounting, funds acquisition, etc.), production planning, distribution, manufacturing, etc. "Business processes can be identified to describe the major activities performed and decisions made by the business in the course of managing its resources throughout their life cycles." Since each process uses or creates data, it is possible to construct an *information architecture* matrix that depicts the organization's basic processes, the data used or created by each, and the information systems needed to support or automate them.

BSP, the general-purpose information system planning methodology, aims at covering the waterfront of application opportunities. It has no reason to exclude a priori any information system variety. Why then the following injunction to those who participate in BSP studies as interviewers of top executives:

> Explain environment as being those things that are external to the scope of the BSP study and over which management has little or no control?

And what does BSP see when it looks at the environment?

> Environment (defined as those things outside the scope of the study and over which the business has little or no control)—economy, *government regulations, labor,* consumerism, *competition,* industry position and *industry trends, suppliers,* and *technology.* [Italics added.][35]

The italicized items represent possible targets and opportunity areas for SIS and SIS alliances. Why has BSP stipulated that they are "outside the scope of the study"? The only explanation I find satisfying is that those who formulated the BSP methodology were captives, in the thrall of Anthony's paradigm. They believed, and were supported by some of the most influential thinkers in the information management field (Zani, Gorry, Scott Morton, Keen, Nolan, King, and Rockart), that there were basically only two kinds of information systems application opportunities, MIS and MSS. Why? Because Anthony's paradigm had narrowed their vision, had blinded them to the new world of SIS opportunities lying over the horizon. To see the objects in this world, a new perspective is needed.

CONCLUSION

I have attempted to show that beneath the conventional gospel on information systems, lies an analytical framework that has

(1) captured the allegiance of a community dedicated to its articulation and (2) governed the design of tools (instruments) to explore the world from the perspective it supports. Analytical frameworks with these properties have come to be known as *paradigms*, after the work of Kuhn in the philosophy of science.

The adoption of Anthony's paradigm contributed significantly to the development of the information management discipline. Researchers, consultants, and practitioners refined and expanded the paradigm to cover new cases. This process of *paradigm articulation* is reflected in the landmark works summarized above.

But the further development of the information management discipline requires a new conceptual foundation, as the conventional perspective (based as it is on the planning and control model) can't account for SIS opportunities. By concentrating its efforts on the narrow range of objects sanctioned by the paradigm, it necessarily precludes other entities that fail to meet its stringent entrance requirements, its criteria for existence. The rejected, the exceptional, the novelties that the paradigm refuses to admit, are the sorts of things that (if perceived by members of the community) cause sleepless nights. These are the objects the paradigm can't handle, the objects that prove its incompleteness, its inability to account for the reality it is supposed to explain.

Ever since the advent of computer processing some 30 years ago, the overwhelming majority of those responsible for thinking about applications has embraced some form of the conventional perspective on systems. The members of this diverse group—ranging from top managers and end users to computer specialists, consultants, and academics in the information management field—have never focused their attention on discovering SIS opportunities.

Puzzling as this may appear at first sight, it can be explained, I believe, quite simply. With these practitioners, SIS have no ontological status. Not existing as objects to be identified, SIS form no part of their horizon of expectation, their mental set, when they search for opportunities to apply computer technology. Is this surprising? Not to one who understands the ontological commitments of the conventional perspective. This viewpoint countenances only two generic varieties of information systems: management information systems (MIS) and management support systems (MSS), the latter comprising the species of decision support systems (DSS) and executive information systems (EIS). (See Appendix B.) To account for SIS requires another perspective on information systems—the strategic.

B

Varieties of Information Systems

INFORMATION SYSTEMS: FUNCTION
AND USE

This appendix characterizes the major varieties of information systems and points out the environmental conditions contributing to their emergence and growth. Let us agree at the outset to understand the term *information system* broadly as a computer-based system capable of serving organizational purposes. This definition allows us to distinguish varieties of information systems in terms of their technical functions and organizational uses.

The distinction between an object's *use* and its *function* applies not only to information systems but to other complex and diverse entities as well. Take airplanes, for example. Like many technological wonders, they have multiple uses: Prior to World War I, they were used exclusively as recreational and sporting vehicles. During the war, they were used primarily for scouting purposes behind enemy lines. After the war, the first commercial use of aircraft was established. The Post Office Department created airmail routes, first between New York and Washington and then across the country. The next major use of aircraft was as transportation vehicles, which led to the formation of the commercial carrier fleets that we are accustomed to today. In the military sphere, the use of aircraft evolved from scouting to systematic aerial reconnaissance, routine bombing, transport, etc. The military counts these uses of aircraft as *conventional* to distinguish them from their various *strategic* missions.

When talking of the functional features of an airplane, I have in mind such elements as speed, capacity, maneuverability, and distance. Combining the categories of use and function allows us to distinguish various classes of aircraft (for example, fighter planes from transports) in terms of their respective technical functions and intended uses.

Now, the distinction between use and function on the one hand and conventional and strategic on the other may be applied in the information management field as well. It is my contention that information systems have multiple uses and that some of these are conventional and some are strategic. Just as it took the military a long time to appreciate the strategic significance of some weapon systems, so too it has taken the business community a long time to appreciate the strategic significance of information systems. To see this, one must first be clear about the conventional varieties of information systems, MIS and MSS.

MANAGEMENT INFORMATION SYSTEMS

The term *management information systems* has never been defined to everyone's satisfaction. At one point in its early history, it meant for some what most today would call "decision support" or "executive information systems." But it has also had other definitions. In the late 60s and early 70s, MIS were frequently considered to be those systems that did not provide the information needed or wanted by management. After the framework proposed by Anthony Gorry and Michael Scott Morton for decision support systems (see Appendix A), MIS began to be viewed as those applications not counted as decision support systems. This is roughly the sense I am trying to capture here.

Management information systems (see Figure B–1) may be defined as information systems that have as their primary function the processing of predefined transactions to produce fixed-format reports on schedule. Their principal use is to automate the basic business processes of the organization. Typical transactions handled by MIS are payroll records, customer orders, purchase requests, and the like. MIS were the first information system variety to blossom, taking root easily in the fertile financial and accounting soil of large firms. It took no great conceptual leap on the part of MIS pioneers to conclude, after observing a room full of payroll clerks performing calculations, that here was a good opportunity to use the new technology.

In this initial period of explosive growth, the objective was to replace the manual with the automated. Information system application opportunities were identified by inspection, by observation. As time went on, MIS were developed in other areas: manufacturing, purchasing, marketing, and so on.

MIS sufficed when the environmental challenge was to employ the new computer technology to automate manual operations, to develop efficient applications that could reduce or avoid organizational costs. But from the viewpoint of managers or professionals, such systems were frequently judged to be irrelevant, failing to satisfy their information needs. They looked at the explosive growth of MIS and found many systems wanting, unable to support purchasing or scheduling decisions, incapable of producing ad hoc reports, etc. This rising managerial and professional demand for information systems–based support in decision making, coupled with advances in information processing technology, led to the emergence of management support systems, a variety that includes decision support systems and executive information systems as its two main species.

MANAGEMENT SUPPORT SYSTEMS

The primary function of management support systems (see Figure B–1), by definition, is to provide end users with query and anal-

Figure B-1   Varieties of information systems

Use \\ Function	Automating basic processes	Satisfying information needs	Supporting or shaping competitive strategy
Transaction processing	MIS	/////	SIS
Query and analysis	/////	MSS	SIS

ysis capabilities. The principal use of MSS is to satisfy the information needs of managers and professionals, needs often closely connected with decision making. Typical query and analysis functions are: searching a data base for an item of information, generating what-if scenarios to test implications of planning models, and so on.

Within the past five years, the use of information systems by managers and professionals has grown exponentially, stimulated by the increasing supply of software tools for end-user computing available on mainframes, micros, and through outside time-sharing services. MSS development and demand show no signs of abating.

The tasks supported by MSS are often ill-defined. While some MSS do automate tasks previously performed manually, others reflect creative applications often developed by end users who, for the first time, have been given the computer power to experiment. Also contributing to the avalanche of MSS applications has been the availability of microcomputer software like Visicalc and Lotus 1-2-3, fourth-generation time-sharing languages like Focus and Ramis, and financial planning packages like IFPS and Express.

The emergence of MSS signals the diversification of the information management business into a new product line, with new technology, new customer groups, and new customer needs to be attended to. Unlike MIS, MSS depend primarily on time-sharing and, more recently, on microcomputer technology. The MSS target groups are managers and professionals rather than the clerical and operational markets served by MIS. MSS satisfy the needs of decision makers and professionals for information. With MSS, the definition of the information management business changes as it expands its scope along the dimensions just mentioned.

It is interesting to note that many MIS veterans resisted the emergence of MSS, refusing to admit their existence. Some claimed that MSS were merely extensions of well-conceived MIS. Others argued that MSS were the cream and MSS developers just skimmers. But none of these objections could stem the tide bringing waves of new MSS applications. By the early 80s, demand for MSS far outstripped the demand for MIS applications.

The emergence of this new information system variety brought with it a different group of information system developers, developers not only trained in the intricacies of information technology but also skilled in business disciplines like logistics, inventory control, and strategic planning. Many MSS developers had backgrounds in management science/operations research. They differed culturally from their MIS colleagues, having different career goals, different views about the role of computers in the organization, and different degrees of interest in information processing technology.

To be an MSS developer, one must be willing and able to empathize with business managers and professionals who cannot always specify their requirements with the degree of precision expected by MIS designers. Unlike the MIS pioneers who relied on observation, the MSS vanguard who aid end users (and not all MSS are built by developers trained in this line of work) often must draw upon their conceptual understanding of the decision-making process, frequently unobservable.

Just as the unmet information needs of managers and professionals present MSS opportunities, the savage competitive forces of the 80s—unleashed by deregulation, foreign competition, and accelerated product change, for example—open up SIS opportunities. Just as MSS extend the use of information systems beyond the automation of basic business processes, the recent emergence of SIS (the newest information system variety) extends the use of information systems still further.

STRATEGIC INFORMATION SYSTEMS

By definition, strategic information systems (see Figure B-1) are information systems in which the primary function of the system is either to process predefined transactions and produce fixed-format reports on schedule or to provide query and analysis capabilities. The primary use of SIS is to support or shape the competitive strategy of the organization, its plan for gaining (or maintaining) competitive advantage.

SIS represents a new information management product line, targeting new user groups, satisfying new user needs—needs unsatisfied by MIS or MSS and often requiring new technologies. Like the emergence of MIS, the emergence of SIS forces the information management group to redefine its business and its goals. The scope of information management activities is again extended.

With extended scope and a clearer sense of the tasks imposed by the existence of SIS, organizations must turn their attention to implementation issues such as personnel, organization, and culture. Adjustments must be made to accommodate the new SIS product line. The sorts of actions taken to further the growth of MSS must be repeated for SIS.

With the emergence of SIS, emphasis switches from function to use. What is critical is the use of information systems to support or shape strategy rather than the capability to process transactions or do query and analysis. SIS planners must discover application opportunities through reflection, by thinking about how the use of information systems can enable the organization to gain a competitive advantage. Unlike their MIS counterparts, they cannot rely on observation alone.

HYBRID INFORMATION SYSTEMS

To avoid possible confusions about applying the taxonomy just introduced, note that the two dimensions of an information system, technical function and organizational use, each comprise overlapping categories. Hence the possibility of *hybrid* information systems—MIS/MSS, MIS/SIS, and MIS/MSS/SIS—appearing at the MIS, MSS, and SIS intersections in Figure B–2.

For example, American's Sabre reservation system is an MIS/SIS hybrid. RCA's human resource management system, IRIS, is an MIS/MSS hybrid. In its MIS use, IRIS records significant events in the history of each RCA employee and generates standard, usually mandatory, reports periodically. In its MSS use, IRIS permits RCA executives to query and analyze its data base when information is

Figure B-2   Information system hybrids

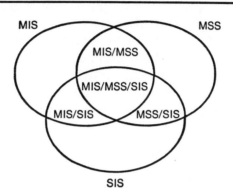

needed to support decisions concerning project team composition, training budgets, and so on.

Keep in mind when applying this taxonomy that an information system may, from the point of view of its organizational developer, be classed as an SIS, but from the perspective of an external user, it may be taken as an MSS, MIS, or MIS/MSS hybrid. The Metpath information system mentioned earlier illustrates this situation. For Metpath, it is an SIS; for the physicians using it, it is an MIS, or perhaps even an MIS/MSS hybrid.

CONVENTIONAL VERSUS STRATEGIC WEAPONS

Let me close this section by suggesting a dramatic way of drawing the distinction between MIS and MSS on the one hand and SIS on the other. Think of MIS and MSS as conventional weapons, like fighter planes or destroyers, and SIS as strategic weapons, like long-range bombers capable of hitting strategic targets (e.g., urban-industrial complexes, nuclear-launching sites) in the enemy's heartland. According to U.S. government doctrine, a weapon is

counted as strategic if it plays a central role in support of fundamental politico-military policies such as deterrence or retaliation.

To manage and operate the strategic arsenal, special organizations dedicated to the task are needed. The Joint Strategic Target
Planning Staff (JSTPS), a high-level Defense Department group, is
assigned to draw up a "National Strategic Target List" and prepare a
"Single Integrated Operating Plan" to guide the interservice coordination of strategic weapons. The Strategic Air Command (SAC), a
special force of B–52 bombers carrying nuclear weapons, is responsible for deterring the Soviet Union from attacking the United
States.

In the business sphere, SIS plays a role vis-à-vis the organization's strategy similar to the one played by strategic weapons vis-à-
vis the U.S. government's politico-military policies. Both are used
to support and shape policy/strategy. When information systems
are used in this fashion, to support or shape the organization's
strategy, they should be viewed as *competitive weapons*. As such,
these SIS may require the formation of special groups, like the
JSTPS or the SAC just mentioned, to manage or operate them. (See
Chapter 8 for more on this subject.)

NOTES

[1]*Dun & Bradstreet Annual Report*, 1979, p. 6.

[2]Ibid., p. 12.

[3]*McKesson Annual Report*, 1983, pp. 2–3.

[4]Ibid., p. 7.

[5]*Banc One Annual Report*, 1983, p. 21.

[6]Ibid., pp. 3–4.

[7]Ibid., p. 23.

[8]*General Motors Annual Report*, 1925.

[9]Alfred D. Chandler, Jr., *Strategy and Structure: Chapters in the History of American Industrial Enterprise* (Cambridge, Mass.: Harvard University Press, 1962), p. 391.

[10]Michael E. Porter, *Competitive Strategy: Techniques for Analyzing Industries and Competitors* (New York: Free Press, 1980), p. 35.

[11]Ibid., p. 37.

[12]Ibid., p. 38.

[13]*Computerworld*, March 12, 1984, p. 8.

[14]*Computerworld*, August 22, 1983, p. 20.

[15]See Ian MacMillan, "Preemptive Strategies," *Journal of Business Strategy*, Fall 1983.

[16]*Information Systems News*, November 16, 1981, p. 28.

[17]*New York Times*, September 22, 1983.

[18]*Electronic Banking: An Executive's Guide*, Citibank, New York, p. 3 (no date).

[19]Quoted in "GE Business Development," Harvard Business School Case Studies: 1982, #4–382–092, revised June 1982, p. 2.

[20]*Datamation*, February 1983, pp. 56–58.

[21]Edith T. Penrose, *The Theory of the Growth of the Firm*. (Oxford: Basil Blackwell, 1959).

[22]See also Arnoldo C. Hax and Nicolas S. Maljuf, *Strategic Management: An Integrative Perspective* (Englewood Cliffs, NJ: Prentice-Hall, 1984); Ian MacMillan, "Preemtive Strategies," *Journal of Business Strategy*, Fall 1983; Michael Porter, *Competitive Strategy: Techniques for Analyzing Industries and Competitors* (New York: Free Press, 1980); Stanley Davis and Howard Schwartz, "Matching Corporate Culture and Business Strategy," *Organizational Dynamics*, Summer 1981.

[23]IBM, *Information Systems Planning Guide: Business Systems Planning*, 3d ed., 1981, p. 82.

[24]Robert N. Anthony, *Planning and Control Systems: A Framework for Analysis* (Cambridge, Mass.: Harvard University Press, 1965), p. 49.

[25]William Zani, "Blueprint for MIS," *Harvard Business Review*, November–December 1970, p. 98.

[26]Richard Nolan and Charles Gibson, "Managing the Four Stages of EDP Growth," *Harvard Business Review*, 1974.

[27]Richard Nolan, "Managing the Crises in Data Processing," *Harvard Business Review*, March–April 1979.

[28]Richard Nolan, "Plight of the EDP Manager," *Harvard Business Review*, May–June 1973.

[29]John Rockart, "Chief Executives Define Their Own Data Needs," *Harvard Business Review*, March–April 1979.

[30]John Rockart and Christine Bullin, "A Primer on Critical Success Factors," *CISR Working Paper*, Sloan School of Management, MIT, 1981.

[31]William King, "Strategic Planning for MIS," *MIS Quarterly*, March 1978.

[32]William King, "Achieving the Potential of Decision Support Systems," *Journal of Business Strategy*, Winter 1983.

[33]Ibid., p. 37.

[34]IBM, *Information Systems Planning Guide*, p. 6.

[35]Ibid., p. 22.

Index of Cases

Subject Index